LANGUAGE ARTS 300
Teacher's Guide

Author:
Alpha Omega Publications

Editor:
Alan Christopherson, M.S.

804 N. 2nd Ave. E.
Rock Rapids, IA 51246-1759

LANGUAGE ARTS 300

LIFEPAC® Overview

LANGUAGE ARTS SCOPE & SEQUENCE

KINDERGARTEN

Lessons 1-40	Lessons 41-80	Lessons 81-120	Lessons 121-160
Alphabet -say the alphabet **Colors** -recognize colors **Directions** -left to right **Following directions** -given once **Grammar** -form simple sentences **Listening skills** **Personal recognition** -read and write first name -know age and address -recognize names of family members **Phonics** -short *a, e, i* vowels -initial: *b, t, m, r, s, n, d, p, l* -form and read simple words -form rhyming words **Shapes** -circle, square, triangle, and rectangle -recognize shapes in objects **Stories and poems** -create simple stories and poems **Writing** -form circles and lines -*Aa, Bb, Dd, Ee, Ii, Ll, Mm, Nn, Pp, Rr, Ss,* and *Tt*	**Grammar** -sentences begin with capital, end with period **Patterns** -simple shape, color patterns **Personal recognition** -read and write first and last name **Phonics** -*short a, e, i, o,* and *u* vowels -initial: *k, c, ck, f, h, g, j, v, w, y, z, qu,* and *x* -read simple sentences **Position/direction concepts** -in/out, in front of/behind, up/down, on/off, open/closed, over/under **Sequencing** -alphabetical order -simple story **Shapes** -oval **Size concepts** -big/little, large/small **Writing** -*Kk, Cc, Ff, Hh, Oo, Gg, Jj, Vv, Ww, Uu, Yy, Zz, Qq,* and *Xx*	**Phonics** -recognize the short vowel sounds -recognize all initial consonant sounds -recognize long *a, e, i, o,* and *u* sounds -silent *e* -initial consonant digraphs: *sh, ch,* both soft and hard *th* -final consonant sounds: *_b, _ck, _k, _l* **Word recognition** -color words, number words and shape words **Writing** -name -complete alphabet, capital and small letters -all color words -number words: *one, two, three, four, five, six* -shape words: *circle, square, triangle*	**Phonics** -recognize the long vowel sounds -initial consonant diagraphs: *wh;* review *ch, sh, th* -recognize all final consonant sounds **Stories and poems** -create, tell, and recite stories and poems **Word recognition** -position/direction words: *up/down, high/low, in/inside, out/outside, top/bottom* -number words: *seven, eight, nine, ten* -shape words: *rectangle, oval, star* **Writing** -number words: *seven, eight, nine, ten* -shape words: *rectangle, oval, star* -position/direction words: *up/down, high/low, in/inside, out/outside, top/bottom*

LANGUAGE ARTS SCOPE & SEQUENCE

	Alphabet Sounds (Grade 1)	The Parts of Speech (Grade 2)	Reading Skills (Grade 3)
Unit 1	**ALPHABET AND SHORT VOWEL SOUNDS** • Short vowel sounds • Consonants • Main ideas • Rhyming words	**KNOW YOUR NOUNS** • Review vowels and consonants • Beginning, middle, and ending sounds • Singular and plural nouns • Common and proper nouns	**OLD AND NEW SKILLS** • Vowels and consonants • Sentence phrases • Capital letters • Reading skills
Unit 2	**RHYMING WORDS, ADDING "ING"** • Kinds of sentences • Cardinal and ordinal numbers • Suffixes and plurals • Classifying	**ACTION VERBS** • Vowel digraphs • Action words - verbs • Following directions • The dictionary • ABC order	**BUILDING WORDS AND SENTENCES** • Long and short vowels • Questions • ABC order • Capital letters
Unit 3	**CONSONANT DIGRAPHS, SOFT C AND G** • Consonant digraphs • Compounds and syllables • Possessives and contractions • Soft c and g	**SIMPLE SENTENCES** • R-controlled vowels • Consonant blends • Using capital letters • Subjects and verbs in sentences	**WORDS: GETTING TO THE ROOTS** • Root words • Dictionary guide words • Synonyms and antonyms • Capital letters
Unit 4	**VERBS, BLENDS, AND SILENT LETTERS** • Paragraphs • Silent letters • Sequencing • Subject-verb agreement	**TYPES OF SENTENCES** • Consonant digraphs • Statement, question, and exclamatory sentences • Using capital letters • The library	**WORDS: HOW TO USE THEM** • Noun and verb • Adjective and adverb • Irregular vowels • Composition
Unit 5	**LONG VOWELS AND SYLLABLES** • Long vowels and homonyms • Syllables, possessives, and contractions • Plurals and suffixes • Poetry	**USING PUNCTUATION** • Diphthongs • Punctuation review • Contractions • Rules for making words plural • Writing a biography	**SENTENCE: START TO FINISH** • Main idea • Capital letters and punctuation • Paragraphs • Making words plural
Unit 6	**R-CONTROLLED VOWELS AND PLURALS** • R-controlled vowels • Writing stories • Pronouns • Following directions	**ADJECTIVES** • Rhyming words • Biblical poetry • Synonyms and antonyms • Adjectives in sentences • Comparative and superlative adjectives	**ALL ABOUT BOOKS** • Main idea • Books • Stories • Poems • Critical thinking
Unit 7	**VOWEL DIGRAPHS AND SENTENCES** • Vowel digraphs • Letters — business, friendly, invitations • Syllables	**POSSESSIVE NOUNS** • Introduction to letter writing • Pronunciation key • Possessive nouns • Silent consonants • Homonyms	**READING AND WRITING** • For directions • Friendly letters • Pronouns • Fact and fiction
Unit 8	**VOWEL DIGRAPHS AND POSSESSIVES** • Vowel digraphs • Subject-verb agreement • Compounds and contractions • Possessives • Pronoun	**PRONOUNS** • Author's intent and use of titles • Predicting content • Character, setting, and plot • Analogies • Writing in cursive	**READING SKILLS** • For sequence • For detail • Being and compound verbs • Drama
Unit 9	**DIPHTHONGS AND CONTRACTIONS** • Vowel digraphs • Titles and main ideas • Sentences and paragraphs • Proper nouns	**VERB TYPES AND TENSES** • Review action verbs • Dividing words into syllables • State of being verbs • Past and present verb tenses	**MORE READING AND WRITING** • For information • Thank-you letters • Book reports • Reference books
Unit 10	**PHONICS AND GRAMMAR REVIEW** • Letters and sounds • Contractions • Plurals and possessives • Sentences • Stories	**LOOKING BACK** • Nouns and verbs • Word division • Consonant blends and digraphs • Prefixes, suffixes, and root words • Possessives, pronouns, and adjectives	**LOOKING BACK** • Reading for comprehension • Sentence punctuation • Writing letters • Parts of speech

LANGUAGE ARTS SCOPE & SEQUENCE

Written Communication and Fiction (Grade 4)	Story Elements and Poetry (Grade 5)	Reading for a Purpose (Grade 6)	
WRITTEN COMMUNICATION • Word derivations • Story sequence • Writing an outline • Writing a report	STORY MESSAGES • Main idea and plot • Character and setting • Dialogue • Diphthongs • Digraphs	READING FOR A PURPOSE • Critical thinking • Research data • Parables • Synonyms	Unit 1
SOUNDS TO WORDS • Hard and soft — c and g • Parts of a dictionary • Accented syllables • Haiku poetry	MAIN IDEAS • Poetry and stories • Synonyms • Topic sentences • Adjectives and nouns • Compounds	FORMING NEW WORDS • Prefixes and suffixes • Synonyms and antonyms • Adjectives and adverbs • Critical thinking	Unit 2
WORDS: HOW TO USE THEM • Prefixes and suffixes • Homonyms and antonyms • Poetry and stories • Writing an outline	WORDS TO STORIES • Subject and predicate • Adverbs • Critical thinking • Writing a short story • Idioms	BETTER READING • Story elements • Author's purpose • Information sources • Outline	Unit 3
MORE WORDS: HOW TO USE THEM • Parts of speech • Written directions • Verb tenses • Possessives	WRITTEN REPORT • Outline • Metaphor and simile • Writing the report • Types of sentences	SENTENCES • Capitals and punctuation • Author's purpose • Propaganda • Types of sentences	Unit 4
WRITING FOR CLARITY • Figures of speech • Capital letters • Punctuation marks • Writing stories	STORY ELEMENTS • Legend • Dialogue and quotations • Word order and usage • Story elements • Implied meaning	READING SKILLS • Following directions • Literary forms • Phrases, nouns, and verbs • Paragraph structure	Unit 5
FUN WITH FICTION • Book reports • Fiction and nonfiction • Parables and fables • Poetry	POETRY • Rhythm • Symbolism • Personification • Irregular plurals • Stanza	POETRY • Similes and metaphors • Alliteration and homonyms • Palindromes • Figures of speech • Acronyms	Unit 6
FACT AND FICTION • Nouns and verbs • Contractions • Biography • Tall tales • Fables	WORD USAGE • Common, plural, and possessive nouns • Fact and opinion • Story and main idea	STORIES • Story elements • Nouns and pronouns • Vowel digraphs • Business letters	Unit 7
GRAMMAR AND WRITING • Adjectives to compare • Adverbs • Figurative language • Paragraphs	ALL ABOUT VERBS • Tense and action • Participles • Regular and irregular • Singular and plural	ANALYZING THE NEWS • Propaganda • News stories • Auxiliary verbs and verb tenses • Adverbs	Unit 8
THE WRITTEN REPORT • Planning a report • Finding information • Creating an outline • Writing a report	READING FLUENCY • Speed reading • Graphic aids • Study skills • Literary forms	READING THE BIBLE • Parables and proverbs • Hebrew poetry and prophecy • Bible history • Old Testament law	Unit 9
LOOKING BACK • Reading skills • Nouns and adverbs • Written communication • Literary forms	LOOKING BACK • Literary forms • Parts of speech • Writing skills • Study skills	LOOKING BACK • Literary forms • Writing letters • Parts of speech • Punctuation	Unit 10

LANGUAGE ARTS SCOPE & SEQUENCE

	Grammar and Nonfiction (Grade 7)	Speaking and Writing Skills (Grade 8)	English I (Grade 9)
Unit 1	**WORD USAGE** • Proper and common nouns • Pronouns • Prefixes and suffixes • Synonyms and antonyms	**IMPROVING COMMUNICATION** • Roots and inflections • Affixes and interjections • Oral and written directions • Non-verbal communication	**THE STRUCTURE OF LANGUAGE** • Nouns, adjectives, and prepositions • Verbs, adverbs, and conjunctions • Sentence parts • Diagram sentences
Unit 2	**MORE WORD USAGE** • Speech: Stress and pitch • Verb tenses • Principle parts	**ALL ABOUT ENGLISH** • Origin of language • Classification of nouns, pronouns, verbs, adjectives, and adverbs	**NATURE OF LANGUAGE** • Origin of language • Using oral and written language • Dictionary • Writing a paper
Unit 3	**BIOGRAPHIES** • Biography as a form • Flashback technique • Deductive reasoning • Base and root words	**PUNCTUATION AND LITERATURE** • Connecting and interrupting • The essay • Thesis statement	**PRACTICAL ENGLISH** • Dictionary use • Mnemonics • Writing a paper • Five-minute speech
Unit 4	**STRUCTURE OF LANGUAGE** • Verb tenses • Principle parts • Sentence creativity • Speech: Pitch and accent	**WORDS AND HOW TO USE THEM** • Dictionary • Thesaurus • Accent and diacritical marks • Standard and nonstandard	**READING WITH SKILL** • Plot and setting • Characterization • Conflict • Symbolism
Unit 5	**THE NATURE OF ENGLISH** • Formal and informal • Redundant expressions • Verb tenses • Subject-verb agreement	**CORRECT LANGUAGE USAGE** • Using good form • Synonyms and antonyms • Homonyms • Good speaking qualities	**LANGUAGE IN LITERATURE** • Collective nouns and verbs • Use of comparisons • Gerunds and participles • Literary genres
Unit 6	**THE MECHANICS OF ENGLISH** • Punctuation • Complements and modifiers • Subordinate and coordinate clauses	**LANGUAGE AND LITERATURE** • History of English • Coordination and Subordination • Autobiography	**STRUCTURE AND MEANING IN PROSE AND POETRY** • Author's purpose and meaning • Meaning of structure • Factors of persuasion • Understanding poetry
Unit 7	**THE HIDING PLACE: A STUDY GUIDE** • Sequence of events • Facts about characters • Author's purpose • Character sketch	**CRITICAL READING AND PARAGRAPH SKILLS** • Word evaluation • The paragraph: Structure, coherence, introduction, and conclusion	**COMMUNICATION** • Planning a speech • Listening comprehension • Business, informal, and social letters
Unit 8	**LITERATURE** • Nonfiction • Listening skills • Commas and semicolons • Nonverbal communication	**WRITING, LISTENING, AND READING** • Business letters • Personal letters • Four steps to listening • Nonfiction	**THE LIBRARY AND DRAMA** • Library resources • Drama: History, elements, and reading • *The Miracle Worker*
Unit 9	**COMPOSITIONS** • Sentence types • Quality of paragraphs • Pronunciation • Nonsense literature	**SPEAK AND WRITE** • Etymology • Modifiers • Number and tense • Oral report	**STUDIES IN THE NOVEL** • History and definition • Critical essay • *Twenty Thousand Leagues Under the Sea*
Unit 10	**LOOKING BACK** • Parts of speech • Sentence structure • Punctuation • How to communicate	**LANGUAGE ELEMENTS IN REVIEW** • Composition structure • Parts of speech • Critical thinking • Literary forms	**LOOKING BACK** • Communication: Writing, speaking, and listening • Using resources • Literature review • Diagram sentences

LANGUAGE ARTS SCOPE & SEQUENCE

English II (Grade 10)	English III (Grade 11)	English IV (Grade 12)	
THE DEVELOPMENT OF ENGLISH • Historical development • Varieties of English • Substandard and standard • Changes in English	**STANDARD ENGLISH** • Need for standard English • Guardians of the standard • Dictionaries • Types of standard English texts	**THE WORTH OF WORDS** • Word categories • Expository writing • Sentence structure • Diction	Unit 1
LISTENING AND SPEAKING • Noun plurals • Suffixes • Creating a speech • Nature of listening	**WRITING EFFECTIVE SENTENCES** • Subordinate clauses and conjunctions • Relative pronouns • Verbals • Appositives	**THE STRUCTURE OF LANGUAGE** • Parts of speech • Sentence structure • Subordinate phrases • Subordinate clauses	Unit 2
WRITING EFFECTIVE SENTENCES • Participles and infinitives • Prepositions and gerunds • Simple, compound, and complex sentences • Diagram sentences	**CLEAR CONNECTIONS: A WRITING WORKSHOP** • Understanding pronouns • Using pronouns correctly • Using modifiers correctly • Parallel sentence structures	**READ, RESEARCH, AND LISTEN** • Reading skills • Resources for research • Taking notes • Drawing conclusions	Unit 3
THE POWER OF WORDS • Etymology • Poetic devices • Literal, figurative, and symbolic poetry • Connotations	**WHY STUDY READING?** • Greek and Latin roots • Diacritical markings • Finding the main idea • Analyzing a textbook	**THE GIFT OF LANGUAGE** • Biblical origin • Koine Greek • Purpose of grammar • Semantics	Unit 4
ELEMENTS OF COMPOSITION • Paragraphs • Connectives and transitions • Elements and ideas of expository writing	**POETRY** • Metrical feet and sets • Musical effects • Universality • Imagery • Connotation	**MEDIEVAL ENGLISH LITERATURE** • Early England • Medieval England • Fourteenth century • Chaucer	Unit 5
STRUCTURE AND READING • Subordinate clauses • Pronouns: Gender, case, and agreement • Reading for recognition	**NONFICTION** • Elements • Essays, diaries, newspapers, and biographies • Composition	**ELIZABETHAN LITERATURE** • Poetry • Prose • Drama • Essay	Unit 6
ORAL READING AND DRAMA • Skills of oral reading • Drama: History, irony, elements, and allegory • *Everyman*	**AMERICAN DRAMA** • Development and history • Structure • Purpose • *Our Town*	**17TH AND 18TH CENTURY ENGLISH LITERATURE** • Historical background • Puritan literature • Common sense and satire • Sensibility	Unit 7
THE SHORT STORY • Elements • Enjoying short stories • Writing • The literary critique	**STUDIES IN THE AMERICAN NOVEL** • Eighteenth, nineteenth, and twentieth century • *The Old Man and the Sea* • The critical essay	**CREATIVE WRITING** • Fundamentals • Inspiration • Technique and style • Form and process	Unit 8
THE NOVEL • Elements • *In His Steps* • The critical essay • The book review	**RESEARCH** • Using sources • Stating the thesis • Outline • Writing the paper	**ROMANTIC AND VICTORIAN POETRY** • Wordsworth and Coleridge • Gordon, Byron, and Shelley • Keats, Tennyson, and Hopkins • Robert and Elizabeth B. Browning	Unit 9
LOOKING BACK • Writing skills • Speech skills • Poetry • Short stories and novels • Drama	**REVIEWING COMMUNICATION SKILLS AND LITERATURE** • Analyzing written word • Effective sentences • Expository prose • Genres of American literature	**LANGUAGE AND ENGLISH LITERATURE REVIEW** • Creative writing • English literature: Medieval to Victorian	Unit 10

STRUCTURE OF THE LIFEPAC CURRICULUM

The LIFEPAC curriculum is conveniently structured to provide one Teacher's Guide containing teacher support material with answer keys and ten student worktexts for each subject at grade levels 2 through 12. The worktext format of the LIFEPACs allows the student to read the textual information and complete workbook activities all in the same booklet. The easy-to-follow LIFEPAC numbering system lists the grade as the first number(s) and the last two digits as the number of the series. For example, the Language Arts LIFEPAC at the 6th grade level, 5th book in the series would be LAN0605.

Each LIFEPAC is divided into three to five sections and begins with an introduction or overview of the booklet as well as a series of specific learning objectives to give a purpose to the study of the LIFEPAC. The introduction and objectives are followed by a vocabulary section which may be found at the beginning of each section at the lower levels or in the glossary at the high school level. Vocabulary words are used to develop word recognition and should not be confused with the spelling words introduced later in the LIFEPAC. The student should learn all vocabulary words before working the LIFEPAC sections to improve comprehension, retention, and reading skills.

Each activity or written assignment in grades 2 through 12 has a number for easy identification, such as 1.1. The first number corresponds to the LIFEPAC section and the number to the right of the decimal is the number of the activity.

Teacher checkpoints, which are essential to maintain quality learning, are found at various locations throughout the LIFEPAC. The teacher should check 1) neatness of work and penmanship, 2) quality of understanding (tested with a short oral quiz), 3) thoroughness of answers (complete sentences and paragraphs, correct spelling, etc.), 4) completion of activities (no blank spaces), and 5) accuracy of answers as compared to the answer key (all answers correct).

The self test questions in grades 2 through 12 are also number coded for easy reference. For example, 2.015 means that this is the 15th question in the self test of Section 2. The first number corresponds to the LIFEPAC section, the zero indicates that it is a self test question, and the number to the right of the zero the question number.

The LIFEPAC test is packaged at the center of each LIFEPAC. It should be removed and put aside before giving the booklet to the student for study.

Answer and test keys in grades 2 through 12 have the same numbering system as the LIFEPACs. The student may be given access to the answer keys (not the test keys) under teacher supervision so that he can score his own work.

A thorough study of the Scope & Sequence by the teacher before instruction begins is essential to the success of the student. The teacher should become familiar with expected skill mastery and understand how these grade-level skills fit into the overall skill development of the curriculum. The teacher should also preview the objectives that appear at the beginning of each LIFEPAC for additional preparation and planning.

TEST SCORING AND GRADING

Answer keys and test keys give examples of correct answers. They convey the idea, but the student may use many ways to express a correct answer. The teacher should check for the essence of the answer, not for the exact wording. Many questions are high level and require thinking and creativity on the part of the student. Each answer should be scored based on whether or not the main idea written by the student matches the model example. "Any Order" or "Either Order" in a key indicates that no particular order is necessary to be correct.

Most self tests and LIFEPAC tests at the lower elementary levels are scored at 1 point per answer; however, the upper levels may have a point system awarding 2 to 5 points for various answers or questions. Further, the total test points will vary; they may not always equal 100 points. They may be 78, 85, 100, 105, etc.

Example 1

Example 2

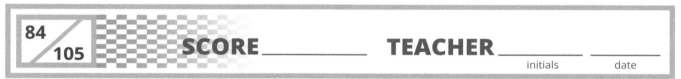

A score box similar to ex. 1 above is located at the end of each self test and on the front of the LIFEPAC test. The bottom score, 72, represents the total number of points possible on the test. The upper score, 58, represents the number of points your student will need to receive an 80% or passing grade. If you wish to establish the exact percentage that your student has achieved, find the total points of his correct answers and divide it by the bottom number (in this case 72). For example, if your student has a point total of 65, divide 65 by 72 for a grade of 90%. Referring to ex. 2, on a test with a total of 105 possible points, the student would have to receive a minimum of 84 correct points for an 80% or passing grade. If your student has received 93 points, simply divide the 93 by 105 for a percentage grade of 89%. Students who receive a score below 80% should review the LIFEPAC and retest using the appropriate Alternate Test found in the Teacher's Guide.

The following is a guideline to assign letter grades for completed LIFEPACs based on a maximum total score of 100 points.

Example:

LIFEPAC Test	=	60% of the Total Score (or percent grade)
Self Test	=	25% of the Total Score (average percent of self tests)
Reports	=	10% or 10* points per LIFEPAC
Oral Work	=	5% or 5* points per LIFEPAC

*Determined by the teacher's subjective evaluation of the student's daily work.

Example:

LIFEPAC Test Score	=	92%	92 x .60 =	55 points
Self Test Average	=	90%	90 x .25 =	23 points
Reports			=	8 points
Oral Work			=	4 points

TOTAL POINTS	=	90 points

Grade Scale based on point system:

100 – 94	=	A
93 – 86	=	B
85 – 77	=	C
76 – 70	=	D
Below 70	=	F

TEACHER GUIDANCE AND STUDYING TECHNIQUES

LIFEPAC activities are written to check the level of understanding of the preceding text. The student may look back to the text as necessary to complete these activities; however, a student should never attempt to do the activities without reading (studying) the text first. Self tests and LIFEPAC tests are never open book tests.

Language arts activities (skill integration) often appear within other subject curriculum. The purpose is to give the student an opportunity to test his skill mastery outside of the context in which it was presented.

Writing complete answers (paragraphs) to some questions is an integral part of the LIFEPAC curriculum in all subjects. This builds communication and organization skills, increases understanding and retention of ideas, and helps enforce good penmanship. Complete sentences should be encouraged for this type of activity. Obviously, single words or phrases do not meet the intent of the activity, since multiple lines are given for the response.

Review is essential to student success. Time invested in review where review is suggested will be time saved in correcting errors later. Self tests, unlike the section activities, are closed book. This procedure helps to identify weaknesses before they become too great to overcome. Certain objectives from self tests are cumulative and test previous sections; therefore, good preparation for a self test must include all material studied up to that testing point.

The following procedure checklist has been found to be successful in developing good study habits in the LIFEPAC curriculum.

1. Read the introduction and Table of Contents.
2. Read the objectives.
3. Recite and study the entire vocabulary (glossary) list.
4. Study each section as follows:
   a. Read the introduction and study the section objectives.
   b. Read all the text for the entire section, but answer none of the activities.
   c. Return to the beginning of the section and memorize each vocabulary word and definition.
   d. Reread the section, complete the activities, check the answers with the answer key, correct all errors, and have the teacher check.
   e. Read the self test but do not answer the questions.
   f. Go to the beginning of the first section and reread the text and answers to the activities up to the self test you have not yet done.
   g. Answer the questions to the self test without looking back.
   h. Have the self test checked by the teacher.
   i. Correct the self test and have the teacher check the corrections.
   j. Repeat steps a–i for each section.
5. Use the SQ3R method to prepare for the LIFEPAC test.

   Scan the whole LIFEPAC.
   Question yourself on the objectives.
   Read the whole LIFEPAC again.
   Recite through an oral examination.
   Review weak areas.

6. Take the LIFEPAC test as a closed book test.
7. LIFEPAC tests are administered and scored under direct teacher supervision. Students who receive scores below 80% should review the LIFEPAC using the SQ3R study method and take the Alternate Test located in the Teacher's Guide. The final test grade may be the grade on the Alternate Test or an average of the grades from the original LIFEPAC test and the Alternate Test.

GOAL SETTING AND SCHEDULES

Each school must develop its own schedule, because no single set of procedures will fit every situation. The following is an example of a daily schedule that includes the five LIFEPAC subjects as well as time slotted for special activities.

Possible Daily Schedule

8:15 – 8:25	Pledges, prayer, songs, devotions, etc.
8:25 – 9:10	Bible
9:10 – 9:55	Language Arts
9:55 – 10:15	Recess (juice break)
10:15 – 11:00	Math
11:00 – 11:45	History & Geography
11:45 – 12:30	Lunch, recess, quiet time
12:30 – 1:15	Science
1:15 –	Drill, remedial work, enrichment*

*__Enrichment:__ *Computer time, physical education, field trips, fun reading, games and puzzles, family business, hobbies, resource persons, guests, crafts, creative work, electives, music appreciation, projects.*

Basically, two factors need to be considered when assigning work to a student in the LIFEPAC curriculum.

The first is time. An average of 45 minutes should be devoted to each subject, each day. Remember, this is only an average. Because of extenuating circumstances, a student may spend only 15 minutes on a subject one day and the next day spend 90 minutes on the same subject.

The second factor is the number of pages to be worked in each subject. A single LIFEPAC is designed to take three to four weeks to complete. Allowing about three to four days for LIFEPAC introduction, review, and tests, the student has approximately 15 days to complete the LIFEPAC pages. Simply take the number of pages in the LIFEPAC, divide it by 15 and you will have the number of pages that must be completed on a daily basis to keep the student on schedule. For example, a LIFEPAC containing 45 pages will require three completed pages per day. Again, this is only an average. While working a 45-page LIFEPAC, the student may complete only one page the first day if the text has a lot of activities or reports, but go on to complete five pages the next day.

Long-range planning requires some organization. Because the traditional school year originates in the early fall of one year and continues to late spring of the following year, a calendar should be devised that covers this period of time. Approximate beginning and completion dates can be noted on the calendar as well as special occasions such as holidays, vacations and birthdays. Since each LIFEPAC takes three to four weeks or 18 days to complete, it should take about 180 school days to finish a set of ten LIFEPACs. Starting at the beginning school date, mark off 18 school days on the calendar and that will become the targeted completion date for the first LIFEPAC. Continue marking the calendar until you have established dates for the remaining nine LIFEPACs making adjustments for previously noted holidays and vacations. If all five subjects are being used, the ten established target dates should be the same for the LIFEPACs in each subject.

TEACHING SUPPLEMENTS

The sample weekly lesson plan and student grading sheet forms are included in this section as teacher support materials and may be duplicated at the convenience of the teacher.

The student grading sheet is provided for those who desire to follow the suggested guidelines for assignment of letter grades as previously discussed. The student's self test scores should be posted as percentage grades. When the LIFEPAC is completed, the teacher should average the self test grades, multiply the average by .25, and post the points in the box marked self test points. The LIFEPAC percentage grade should be multiplied by .60 and posted. Next, the teacher should award and post points for written reports and oral work. A report may be any type of written work assigned to the student whether it is a LIFEPAC or additional learning activity. Oral work includes the student's ability to respond orally to questions, which may or may not be related to LIFEPAC activities, or any type of oral report assigned by the teacher. The points may then be totaled and a final grade entered along with the date that the LIFEPAC was completed.

The Student Record Book, which was specifically designed for use with the Alpha Omega curriculum, provides space to record weekly progress for one student over a nine-week period as well as a place to post self test and LIFEPAC scores. The Student Record Books are available through the current Alpha Omega catalog; however, unlike the enclosed forms, these books are not for duplication and should be purchased in sets of four to cover a full academic year.

This section of the language arts Teacher's Guide also includes a *Book Report Form*, a *Books Read Chart, Phonics Rules*, and the Index of Concepts. The Book Report Form and the Books Read Chart may be duplicated for individual student use.

The Index of Concepts is a quick reference guide for the teacher who may be looking for a rule or explanation that applies to a particular concept. It does not identify each use of the concept in the various LIFEPACs. The concepts change by grade level with the emphasis on phonics and reading skills for younger students changing to spelling and grammar for the older students.

WEEKLY LESSON PLANNER

Week of:

	Subject	Subject	Subject	Subject
Monday				
Tuesday	Subject	Subject	Subject	Subject
Wednesday	Subject	Subject	Subject	Subject
Thursday	Subject	Subject	Subject	Subject
Friday	Subject	Subject	Subject	Subject

WEEKLY LESSON PLANNER

Week of: _____

	Subject	Subject	Subject	Subject
Monday				
Tuesday	Subject	Subject	Subject	Subject
Wednesday	Subject	Subject	Subject	Subject
Thursday	Subject	Subject	Subject	Subject
Friday	Subject	Subject	Subject	Subject

Student Name _____   Year _____

Bible

LP	Self Test Scores by Sections					Self Test Points	LIFEPAC Test	Oral Points	Report Points	Final Grade	Date
	1	2	3	4	5						
01											
02											
03											
04											
05											
06											
07											
08											
09											
10											

History & Geography

LP	Self Test Scores by Sections					Self Test Points	LIFEPAC Test	Oral Points	Report Points	Final Grade	Date
	1	2	3	4	5						
01											
02											
03											
04											
05											
06											
07											
08											
09											
10											

Language Arts

LP	Self Test Scores by Sections					Self Test Points	LIFEPAC Test	Oral Points	Report Points	Final Grade	Date
	1	2	3	4	5						
01											
02											
03											
04											
05											
06											
07											
08											
09											
10											

Student Name _____   Year _____

Math

LP	Self Test Scores by Sections 1	2	3	4	5	Self Test Points	LIFEPAC Test	Oral Points	Report Points	Final Grade	Date
01											
02											
03											
04											
05											
06											
07											
08											
09											
10											

Science

LP	Self Test Scores by Sections 1	2	3	4	5	Self Test Points	LIFEPAC Test	Oral Points	Report Points	Final Grade	Date
01											
02											
03											
04											
05											
06											
07											
08											
09											
10											

Spelling/Electives

LP	Self Test Scores by Sections 1	2	3	4	5	Self Test Points	LIFEPAC Test	Oral Points	Report Points	Final Grade	Date
01											
02											
03											
04											
05											
06											
07											
08											
09											
10											

BOOK REPORT FORM

Title _____   Your Name _____

Author _____   Date _____

Illustrator _____   Principal Characters _____

Number of Pages _____   _____

Copyright Date _____   _____

Fiction or Nonfiction _____   Setting _____

Summary: A summary gives the important events of a story or book. It skips most of the details but a few make the report more interesting. The summary should be written in complete sentences.

_____

_____

_____

_____

_____

_____

_____

_____

_____

_____

_____

_____

_____

_____

Tell why you did or did not like the book.

_____

_____

_____

_____

_____

_____

_____

_____

Name: _____

Books Read			
Title: Author: Date:	Title: Author: Date:	Title: Author: Date:	Title: Author: Date:
Title: Author: Date:	Title: Author: Date:	Title: Author: Date:	Title: Author: Date:
Title: Author: Date:	Title: Author: Date:	Title: Author: Date:	Title: Author: Date:
Title: Author: Date:	Title: Author: Date:	Title: Author: Date:	Title: Author: Date:
Title: Author: Date:	Title: Author: Date:	Title: Author: Date:	Title: Author: Date:
Title: Author: Date:	Title: Author: Date:	Title: Author: Date:	Title: Author: Date:
Title: Author: Date:	Title: Author: Date:	Title: Author: Date:	Title: Author: Date:
Title: Author: Date:	Title: Author: Date:	Title: Author: Date:	Title: Author: Date:
Title: Author: Date:	Title: Author: Date:	Title: Author: Date:	Title: Author: Date:

LANGUAGE ARTS 300 TEACHER NOTES

The following letter and letter combinations are introduced in Language Arts 100 and continue through LA 300. **The LIFEPAC is noted where the rule is specifically addressed.**

a e i o u

b c d f g h j k l m n p q r s t v w x y z

th wh sh ch, ng nk, ck mb lk gn kn gh

ar er ir or ur, ai ay, au aw, ei ey, ea ee, ie

oa, oo, ew, ou, ow, oi, oy

gh ph, igh

1.	short vowels	-	a (bat) e (bet) i (bit) o (cot) u (but)
2.	long vowels	-	a (bait) e (beat) i (bite) o (coat) u (use)
3.	consonants	-	b d f h j k l m n p r s t v w x z
4.	c and g	-	hard sound before a, o, u
		-	soft sound before e, i
5.	q (qu)	-	always has the sound of kw
6.	y	-	as y (yard)
		-	as e (baby)
		-	as i (cry)
7.	consonant digraphs	-	th, wh, sh, ch
8.	special blends	-	ng (sing) nk (sank)
9.	silent consonants	-	ck (lock)
		-	mb (lamb) lk (talk) gn (sign)
		-	kn (know) gh (though) t (often)
10.	r-controlled vowels	-	ar (car) or (for)
		-	er (her) ir (sir) ur (fur)
11.	vowel digraphs	-	ai, ay as long a (pail) (pay)
		-	au, aw (Paul) (paw)
		-	ei, ey as long a (veil) (they)
		-	ea, ee as long e (beat) (feet)
		-	ie as long e (piece)
			as long i (pie)
		-	oa as long o (boat)
		-	oo long sound (boot)
			short sound (book)
		-	ew as long u (few)
		-	ou as long u (soup)
		-	as "ow" (cloud)*
		-	ow as long o (slow)
			as "ow" (clown)*
		-	oi, oy (boil) (boy)*
12.	letter groups	-	gh, ph as f (laugh) (phone)
		-	igh as long i (sigh)

*sometimes referred to as diphthongs

LANGUAGE ARTS 300 INDEX OF CONCEPTS

CONCEPT	LIFEPAC	SECTION	CONCEPT	LIFEPAC	SECTION
Abbreviations	303	4	vowel digraphs	302	4
	304	3		304	1
Alphabetical Order	302	3		306	3,4
	303	1	w-controlled vowels	304	2
	310	4	y as vowel/consonant	304	4
Antonyms	303	3	Plurals	305	2
Book Report	306	2		306	3
	309	3		307	1,2
Capitalization	301	3	Prefixes	303	2
	302	1,2	Pronunciation Key	304	3
	303	2,3,4	Punctuation	301	4
	306	2		304	3
	310	2		305	3
				310	2
Composition			Reading Skills		
letter-writing	307	4	cause/effect	306	3
	309	2	classifying	309	1
paragraph	308	2	context clues	310	1
	310	4	details	306	1
poem	306	4		308	2
story	302	4		310	3
	303	4	fact/fiction	307	3
Compound Words	307	1	following directions	304	2
Dictionary Skills	303	1		307	4
	304	3	main idea	301	2
Homographs	306	4		305	1
Library Skills	306	2		306	1
Literary Forms				307	1
drama (play)	308	3	predicting outcomes	303	3
parable	306	1		305	2
poetry	306	4		309	3
Parts of Speech			sequence of events	303	3
adjectives	304	1		307	2
	308	1,2		308	1
adverbs	304	2	Reference Books	309	3
	309	1	Root Words	303	2
nouns	304	1		304	4
	307	1	Sentence Structure		
pronouns	307	3	phrase	301	3
verbs	304	2,3	sentence	301	3
	308	3		310	1
Phonics			Suffixes	303	2
consonants	301	1,2		307	3
double consonants	307	2	Syllables	305	1
	308	2	Synonyms	303	4
g-hard and soft	306	2		304	4
irregular vowel teams	304	1,2			
r-controlled vowels	303	1,2			
silent letters	301	4			
	310	1			
vowels	310	1			

INSTRUCTIONS FOR LANGUAGE ARTS

The LIFEPAC curriculum from grades 2 through 12 is structured so that the daily instructional material is written directly into the LIFEPACs. The student is encouraged to read and follow this instructional material in order to develop independent study habits. The teacher should introduce the LIFEPAC to the student, set a required completion schedule, complete teacher checks, be available for questions regarding both content and procedures, administer and grade tests, and develop additional learning activities as desired. Teachers working with several students may schedule their time so that students are assigned to a quiet work activity when it is necessary to spend instructional time with one particular student.

Language arts includes those subjects that develop students' communication skills. The LIFEPAC approach to combining reading, spelling, penmanship, composition, grammar, speech and literature in a single unit allows the teacher to integrate the study of these various language arts subject areas. The variety and scope of the curriculum may make it difficult for students to complete the required material within the suggested daily scheduled time of 45 minutes. Spelling, book reports and various forms of composition may need to be completed during the afternoon enrichment period.

Cursive handwriting is introduced in the second grade LIFEPAC 208, with regular practice following in subsequent LIFEPACs. Diacritical markings are defined in the third grade LIFEPAC 304. A pronunciation key including diacritical markings is provided after the vocabulary word lists in all subjects beginning with LIFEPAC 305.

This section of the language arts Teacher's Guide includes the following teacher aids for each unit: Suggested and Required Material (supplies), Additional Learning Activities, Answer Keys, Alternate LIFEPAC Tests, and LIFEPAC Spelling Tests.

Spelling tests contained in the Teacher's Guide are final spelling tests and should be administered with each Language Arts LIFEPAC test. Many words such as "piece" and "peace" are dependent on meaning for correct spelling. By placing the spelling words in sentences, the spelling tests simplify the teacher's work of properly presenting the correct words from the LIFEPAC spelling lists. The practice spelling tests in each section of each LIFEPAC should be designed by the teacher and are not included in this Guide.

The materials section refers only to LIFEPAC materials and does not include materials which may be needed for the additional learning activities. Additional learning activities provide a change from the daily school routine, encourage the students' interest in learning and may be used as a reward for good study habits.

LANGUAGE ARTS 301

Unit 1: Old and New Skills

TEACHER NOTES

MATERIALS NEEDED FOR LIFEPAC	
Required	Suggested
None	• drawing paper • pictures of Mexico and Mexican people • old magazines • sandpaper • index cards

ADDITIONAL LEARNING ACTIVITIES

Section 1: Symbols

1. Discuss these questions with your class.

    a. What do we mean by cursive writing?

    b. What are vowels?

    c. What are consonants?

    d. What is grammar?

    e. What do we mean by punctuation marks?

    f. What are some of the punctuation marks?

    g. What is word study?

2. Ask students to write a lowercase letter *i* in the air. Make it "Jolly Green Giant" size. Do the same with the other letters in Section 1.

3. Ask students to volunteer to say the vowels and then the consonants.

4. Give each student a page from an old magazine. See how many vowels he can find in a certain length of time. Let him underline them on the page.

5. See how many words that student can find beginning with *i, t, s, r, u, w,* and *e* from any source. Make a list.

6. Have each student write the letters of the alphabet in cursive writing. Look at each letter and see what kind of a picture can be made from that letter. Choose five and make a picture of each.

7. Have the student draw letters on sandpaper. Cut them out. Use them later as practice by tracing the sandpaper letter with the fingers (sometimes with eyes closed).

Section 2: Reading a Story

1. Discuss these questions with your class.

   a. Why did Pedro have to stay inside?

   b. Why were Pedro and the boys having trouble talking?

   c. What was Pedro's problem?

   d. How did Pedro learn to speak his first English words?

2. Display pictures and discuss language differences. Talk about how you might learn some Spanish words if you went to Mexico.

3. Practice writing *l, b, f, h,* and *k* in cursive writing in the air in "Jolly Green Giant" size.

4. Ask students to give the short vowel sound they *hear* when teacher says these words: *bath, hut, hot, drum, heaven, hit, sit, sat, top,* and *seven*.

5. Tell students to draw a picture of Pedro as he waits for the boy riding the bicycle. Be sure to show how he feels by the way you draw his face.

6. Tell students to draw a picture of Pedro riding the bicycle.

7. Ask students to make up sentences using their ten spelling words.

Section 3: Writing Good Sentences

1. Discuss these questions with your class.

   a. What is a sentence?

   b. How can you tell the difference between a sentence and phrase?

   c. What parts must you have to make a complete sentence?

   d. How do we begin a sentence?

   e. Where do we use capital letters in a sentence?

2. Have students write three sentences on their own remembering where to use capital letters. Discuss sentences with volunteers.

3. Practice writing *a, d, o, c, j, g, p, y, q, z,* and *f* in the air. Make them large size.

4. Have a spelling bee. When a child misspells a word ask *him to go* to the end of the line so that he can have another turn. There will be no "winner." Use Spelling Words-1 and -2.

5. Place on the chalkboard designs for the children to use (triangles, circles, flowers, a brick wall). After adapting a design to their liking on their paper, let each child fill in the blanks with a properly written letter. He may color in the closed places to create a pretty picture.

6. Make up a puzzle using Spelling Words-2. Save it to share with the class at another time.

7. Have students think of a word that would begin with each of the handwriting letters. Make a list of these words.

Section 4: Punctuating the End of a Sentence

1. Discuss these questions with your class.

   a. What does it mean when we have silent letters in words?

   b. What two kinds of sentences are there?

   c. What do you put at the end of a sentence that tells something?

   d. What do we put at the end of a sentence that asks something?

2. Have students cut an index card in half, put a period (.) on one card and a question mark on the other punctuation card. Read or tell sentences to them, and ask them to hold up the correct punctuation card.

   Example sentences:

   a. Where are you?

   b. He is tall.

   c. This is our room.

   d. What color is your dress?

   e. Let's play together at recess.

   f. My mom is coming to school.

   g. My grandma is visiting us.

   h. What time is it?

   i. How did you get here?

   j. Why is he crying?

3. Have sentences written on the board, some punctuated correctly and some not. Ask students to number a paper accordingly. Write *yes* on the line if the sentence is correct and *no* if it is not. Let them copy the sentence correctly in cursive handwriting.

   Examples:

a. I am tall?	a.	no
b. Today is Friday.	b.	yes
c. Are we going to the store?	c.	yes

4. Practice the handwriting in the air again.

5. Ask students to write five sentences that tell something and five sentences that ask something. (Check also for capitalization.)

6. Ask students to practice all the handwriting letters in LIFEPAC 301. They may use the whiteboard or lined paper.

Administer the LIFEPAC Spelling Test.

Administer the LIFEPAC Test.

ANSWER KEYS

SECTION 1

1.1–1.7 Teacher check
1.8   a, e, i, o, u
1.9   a, e, i, o, u
1.10   b c d f g h j k l m n p q r s t v w x y z
1.11   b c d f g h j k l m n p q r s t v w x y z
1.12   no
            big dog is black
            yes
1.13   ✓ How to write the cursive u
            ✓ How to write the cursive w
            ☐ What rain is
            ✓ Which letters are called consonants
            ☐ All about dogs
            ✓ We will learn about reading
            ✓ Which letters are vowels
            ✓ How to write i and s in cursive
            ✓ Words can be building blocks
            ✓ Words make sense by themselves

SELF TEST 1

1.01–1.07 Teacher check
1.08   a, e, i, o, u
1.09   Reading is fun.
1.10   The dogs are inside.
1.11   Mary went to school today.

SECTION 2

2.1 ✓ Pedro did not know the language of the other children.

2.2 Examples: mother, father, house, play, bicycle, boy, school, book, write

2.3 Answers will vary.

2.4 Examples:
Location and size of Mexico
Foods of Mexico
Climate of Mexico
Schools of Mexico

2.5 Teacher check

2.6 Teacher check

2.7 a, e, i, o, u

2.8 yes   no
yes   yes

2.9 a, e, i, o, u

2.10 b c d f g h j k l m n p q r s t v w x y z

2.11 open

2.12 hold

2.13 fence

2.14 key

2.15 Teacher check

2.16 10

2.17 no

2.18 Teacher check

2.19 Teacher check

SELF TEST 2

2.01–2.03 Teacher check

2.04 b, c, d, f, g, h, j, k, l, m, n, p, q, r, s, t, v, w, x, y, z

2.05 a, e, i, o, u

2.06 God loves me.

2.07 I love to read.

2.08 We love to read about God.

2.09 Jane gave the blessing at dinner.

2.10 hold in

2.11 short

2.12 sentences.

2.13 Yes

2.14 to finger space.

2.15 lŏp   pĭng   be   pĕg

SECTION 3

3.1   ☐ Big friends.
✓ Friends play.
✓ God loves us.
☐ Pretty yellow flowers.
✓ We love Jesus.

3.2   does not make a sentence.

3.3   do not always make a sentence.

3.4   do

3.5   Capital letters are not at the beginning of the sentences.

3.6   Today is a nice day.

3.7   Yesterday was a rainy day.

3.8   I like sunny days best.

3.9   Look at the book.

3.10   My friend is John Smith.

3.11   Will you help me, Kathy?

3.12   Christmas is Jesus' birthday.

3.13   We love God and Jesus.

3.14   begin

3.15   people's names

3.16   always

3.17   Sam was a boy. He loved to go to school.
Sam learned about God.
Sam learned how God loved him.
Sam loved God.

3.18   Teacher check

3.19–3.29 Teacher check

3.30

Across	Down
1. cost	2. shell
3. belt	4. things
5. hum	7. chin
6. ill	
7. caps	
8. bend	

SELF TEST 3

3.01   no

3.02   no

3.03   yes

3.04   yes

3.05–3.07 Teacher check

3.08   God teaches us how to love.

3.09   Jip is Sam's pet.

3.010   The Bible teaches us to love and obey God.

3.011

	short vowel	long vowel
bend	X	
bat	X	
belt	X	
coat		X
cost	X	
ring	X	
shell	X	

3.012   a, e, i, o, u

3.013   consonant

SECTION 4

4.1	gh
4.2	k
4.3	w
4.4	t
4.5	Teacher check
4.6	light
4.7	patch
4.8	knee
4.9	fight
4.10	right
4.11	match
4.12	write
4.13	Teacher check
4.14	do not
4.15	gh
4.16	k
4.17	t
4.18	Teacher check
4.19	Teacher check
4.20	.
4.21	?
4.22	Walking home is fun.
4.23	Do you know Jesus?
4.24	Who is Moses?
4.25	Boys like to run.
4.26	mark
4.27	?
4.28	.

SELF TEST 4

4.01	yes
4.02	catch, right, knee, light, know
4.03	Teacher check
4.04	Teacher check
4.05	Joseph was a brother.
4.06	How many brothers did Joseph have?
4.07	Joseph prayed to God.
4.08	✓ Sue ran to school.
	☐ The big school.
	☐ All the girls.
	✓ God loves everyone.
4.09	lives next door to me.
4.010	a, e, i, o, u
4.011	God gave us his Son, Jesus.
4.012	Will you help Pete with his spelling test?
4.013	a, e, i, o, u
4.014	consonants
4.015	building

LIFEPAC TEST

1.–11. Teacher check
12. a, e, i, o, u
13. happening
14. fence in
15. unlock
16. God loves all people.
17. (catch) (thing) (hum) (on) (shed)
18. he, no
19. the, tom, no
20. yes
21. we, god's, no
22. they, no
23. ?
24. .
25. .
26. ?
27. Once Pedro learned the language, he could learn about God.

ALTERNATE LIFEPAC TEST

1.–5. Teacher check
6. Teacher check
7. God made all things.
8. Are you going home?
9. b, c, d, f, g, h, j, k, m, n
10. names for God
11. beginning of sentence
12. names of people
13. Example:
God is my heavenly Father.
14. d (i) d
15. t h (e) n
16. s p (e) l l
17.–21. Teacher check; examples:
17. knot
18. patch
19. belt
20. cap
21. shell

SPELLING TEST

1	band	The **band** played my favorite songs.	band
2	beg	Does your dog **beg** for its food?	beg
3	bend	He can **bend** the bar with his hands.	bend
4	brush	Did you **brush** your hair this morning?	brush
5	cloth	We dust the furniture with a **cloth**.	cloth
6	thank	Did you **thank** Mother for the gift?	thank
7	trick	My dog learned a new **trick**.	trick
8	caps	I bought two new baseball **caps**.	caps
9	chin	He bumped his **chin** when he fell.	chin
10	cost	How much does a candy bar **cost**?	cost
11	hum	Can you **hum** that tune?	hum
12	ill	Mary stayed home because she was **ill**.	ill
13	shell	The turtle pulled back into its **shell**.	shell
14	catch	Can you **catch** the ball?	catch
15	fight	My dogs often **fight** over a bone.	fight
16	knee	She scraped her **knee** on the sidewalk.	knee
17	knock	Please **knock** on the door before you come in.	knock
18	light	Please turn off the **light** when you leave the room.	light
19	patch	Mother sewed a **patch** on my torn pants.	patch
20	write	Did you **write** a letter to your friend?	write

LANGUAGE ARTS 301

ALTERNATE LIFEPAC TEST

NAME _____

DATE _____

SCORE _____

$$\frac{31}{39}$$

Each answer = 1 point

Write each letter in cursive handwriting.

1. w _____

2. z _____

3. m _____

4. n _____

5. u _____

Write the small letters of the alphabet in cursive handwriting on the lines below.

6. _____

Draw a circle around the group of words that is a sentence.

7. We he they in out.

God made all things.

Things birds cats dogs.

Write the sentence on the line below. Put a . or a ? at the end.

8. Are you going home _____

_____

- -

_____

Circle all the of the consonants.

9. a b c d e f g h i j k m n o u

Draw a line to show the reason why there is a capital letter in each sentence.

10. We learn of God every day.   ●   names of people

11. This is the end.   ●   names for God

12. My friend is John.   ●   beginning of sentence

On the line below, write a sentence that uses a name for God.

13. _____

- -

_____

Put a box around each consonant and a circle around each vowel.

14. d i d   **15.** t h e n   **16.** s p e l l

Write five spelling words that have a short vowel.

17. _____

18. _____

19. _____

20. _____

21. _____

ALTERNATE SPELLING TEST

1	bend	The boat disappeared around the **bend** in the river.	bend
2	brush	We need a new **brush** to finish the painting.	brush
3	chick	We watched the **chick** hatch from the egg.	chick
4	cloth	Her dress is made of the best **cloth**.	cloth
5	plot	The book had a very interesting **plot**.	plot
6	punch	Who will make the **punch** for our party?	punch
7	trick	The magician taught us his favorite **trick**.	trick
8	belt	The **belt** goes with that dress.	belt
9	cost	Those new skates **cost** too much.	cost
10	end	He lives at the **end** of the block.	end
11	ill	You should stay home when you are **ill**.	ill
12	shell	We found a **shell** on the beach.	shell
13	things	All our **things** were stored in the garage.	things
14	know	Do you **know** where my sweater is?	know
15	knot	Tie a **knot** in the rope.	knot
16	right	We will stay **right** here at home tonight.	right
17	match	The candles were lit with a **match**.	match
18	night	I slept very well last **night**.	night
19	wrong	We got lost when we took the **wrong** road.	wrong
20	wrote	Who **wrote** that book?	wrote

LANGUAGE ARTS 302

Unit 2: Building Words and Sentences

TEACHER NOTES

MATERIALS NEEDED FOR LIFEPAC	
Required	Suggested
None	• white glue • wax paper • tempera paints • tagboard or poster board • clay • finger paint and paper • old magazines

ADDITIONAL LEARNING ACTIVITIES

Section 1: Capital Letters

1. Discuss these questions with your class.

   a. What does the word *symbol* mean?

   b. What letters are vowels?

   c. What letters are consonants?

   d. What vowel sound do you hear in a word that has two consonants and a vowel between (long or short)?

   e. If a word has only one consonant followed by a vowel, is the vowel long or short?

   f. Can you name three things we've learned to capitalize?

2. Ask students to practice each of the lowercase letters on a cursive-lined paper.

3. Have students practice uppercase letters *H, K, Z, N, U, Y, W, Q,* and *V* in the air.

4. Write titles of books on the board incorrectly. Ask students to correct them (on the board or on paper).

5. Have students write three or four spelling words in white glue on wax paper. When glue is dry, brush over the top with paint. When paint is dry, cut out oval shape around words.

6. Have students find a short poem, copy it correctly, and memorize it.

Section 2: Sight Words

1. Discuss these questions with your class.

   a. When we write the name of a holiday what must we remember?

   b. What happened to Jeff's money?

   c. What lesson did Jeff learn about sharing?

   d. Have all people learned to share?

2. Students may again practice capitals *O, D, A, C,* and *E* in the air.

3. Ask students to give names of holidays. Make a chart on tagboard or poster board with these names written correctly.

4. Have students write five uses for capital letters.

5. Have students write and illustrate a story telling about a "sharing time" in their lives.

Section 3: Word Order

1. Discuss these questions with your class.

   a. When do vowel sounds have the short sound in a word?

   b. How can we make a short vowel into a long vowel?

   c. Do we *always* have a long vowel when we have a silent e?

   d. What does *alphabetical* order mean?

   e. How do you put words in alphabetical order?

2. Practice *J, L, S, T, F, I,* and *G* in the air.

3. Write some words on the board. Ask students to mark short vowels and long vowels. Cross out the silent letters.

cape	river	cute	us	find
rat	bite	sat	fade	kite
fat	run	long	came	pin

4. Give each student finger painting materials and have them practice the letters *J, L, S, T, F, I,* and *G.* They may also practice the spelling words while they have the materials.

Section 4: Long and Short Vowels

1. Discuss these questions with your class.

   a. Can you name two ways of making a short vowel sound in a word?

   b. Can you name three ways of making a long vowel sound in a word.

   c. How do you know whether to use *ee* or *ea* to make the long *e* sound?

2. Practice handwriting *P, R,* and *B* in the air.

3. Ask students to find pictures in magazines that they could use to make up a story. Then ask them to write a composition about the picture.

4. Ask students to write a short composition using as many of the spelling words as they can.

5. Ask students to make a word scramble game with each of the spelling words (for example, *beach—chaeb*). Save for class use.

6. Allow students to use clay to roll and make each uppercase letter or use finger paint again.

7. Have students write a composition. It may be a poem or short story. Ask them to illustrate their composition.

Administer the LIFEPAC Spelling Test.

Administer the LIFEPAC Test.

ANSWER KEYS

SECTION 1

1.1–1.8 Teacher check
1.9 a e i o u
1.10 Teacher check
1.11 Teacher check
1.12 a. she b. he c. hi
d. be e. no f. we
g. go h. do i. me
j. so k. capital l. correctly
m. cursive n. symbol o. title
1.13 2, 1, 4, 3
1.14 The fox wants the rabbit to go with him.
The rabbit won't go.
1.15 Teacher check
1.16 picture of a key
1.17 picture of a fence
1.18 ă
1.19 ā
1.20 The little boy is happy.
1.21 The fish—swims in a lake
Mary likes—to skate
Jesus helped—a blind man
1.22 Answers will vary.
1.23 Answers will vary.
1.24 Teacher check
1.25 Horses Are Fun
Little House Prairie
Charlotte's Web
1.26 on, the
1.27 A Lost Penny
A Boy and a Dog
The People of Africa
Jokes
1.28 What Ponies Are
1.29 a. Bible
b. Snow White and the Seven Dwarfs
c. Song of Solomon
d. Pooh and Piglet Go Hunting
e. God's Wonderful World

SELF TEST 1

1.01–1.011 Teacher check
1.012 ✓ God and names for God
☐ time of day
✓ beginning of a sentence
☐ numbers
✓ important words in a title
1.013 be hi go no me
1.014 Vowels
1.015 Consonants

SECTION 2

2.1 & 2.2 Teacher check

2.3
a.	and	b.	are	c.	of
d.	only	e.	the	f.	to
g.	too	h.	two	i.	why
j.	who	k.	you	l.	your
m.	comfort	n.	connect	o.	holiday
p.	section				

2.4 Teacher check

2.5 and, are, of, the, of

2.6 The only reason I can't go is that I am sick.

2.7 My bike would work if only I had a tire.

2.8 I only wish I had a pencil.

2.9 Answers will vary.

2.10 Answers will vary.

2.11 too

2.12 too

2.13 you

2.14 your

2.15 Answers will vary.

2.16 Answers will vary.

2.17
a.	your	e.	Who	i.	The
b.	too	f.	and	j.	two
c.	you	g.	to	k.	of
d.	only	h.	are	l.	Why

2.18 Teacher check; sailboat

2.19 holiday

2.20 comfort

2.21 section

2.22 connect

2.23 Christmas
Easter
Labor Day
Memorial Day
New Year's Day

2.24 Drawings will vary.

2.25 Answers will vary.

2.26 Ellen and Her New Friend

Ellen went Christmas shopping today and met Mary Cox. Mary was new to Ellen's town. Mary said she liked December. Ellen asked Mary to go to church with her. Mary said she would like to go with Ellen. Now Ellen has a new friend. Ellen is glad the Lord gave her a new friend.

2.27 Some children are having a party.
A child is coming through the door.
One child is crying.

2.28 no

2.29 a. wanting more than you need

2.30 b. I cried.

2.31 a. he came in suddenly.

2.32 a. someone or something different and nice.

2.33 sigh

2.34 struggled

2.35 anxious

2.36 ✓ on a bus.

2.37 ✓ Two boys ate his candy bar.

2.38 ✓ John

2.39 ✓ he wanted to share.

2.40 Teacher check

SELF TEST 2

2.01	too
2.02	two
2.03	to
2.04–2.09	Teacher check
2.010	Holidays or special days
2.011	People's names
2.012	God and names for God
2.013	Beginning of a sentence
2.014	Titles of books and poems
2.015	sigh
2.016	greedy
2.017	burst
2.018	share
2.019	anxious
2.020	struggled
2.021	sobbed
2.022	special
2.023	(she) (we) (so) (no)

SECTION 3

3.1–3.4 Teacher check

3.5

cut	she	cage
bath	we	cave
half	go	name
pin	be	knife

3.6   a. short   b. long   c. long

3.7

a. bīte	i. kīte
b. cāme	j. pīne
c. cāpe	k. rīpe
d. cōne	l. ūse
e. cūte	m. copy
f. dīne	n. vowel
g. fāde	o. long
h. fīne	p. short

3.8 Teacher check

3.9 Teacher check

3.10 d e f g h i j k l m n o p q r s t u v w x y z

3.11 abcde

3.12 ape, bird, cat, dog

3.13

a. ant	b. only
bear	paper
dish	rock
egg	snow
fish	tall

3.14 alphabetical order.

3.15 first letter.

3.16 yes

3.17 ice, kite, leaf, nose,

SELF TEST 3

3.01 fence the vowel
3.02 short
3.03 long
3.04 long
3.05 the alphabet
3.06 ✓ b.
3.07–3.012 Teacher check
3.013 We went to church on Easter.
3.014 too
3.015 two
3.016 to
3.017 God loves John.

SECTION 4

4.1–4.3 Teacher check
4.4 long, short, long, long, short
4.5
a.	beach	i.	paid
b.	bead	j.	seed
c.	cheer	k.	speak
d.	clean	l.	speech
e.	float	m.	activity
f.	goat	n.	practice
g.	maid	o.	alphabet
h.	neat	p.	circle

4.6 Teacher check
4.7 Teacher check
4.8 Teacher check

SELF TEST 4

4.01–4.06 Teacher check

4.07 (be) (goat) (meat) (rose)

4.08 ✓ a.   ✓ c.

4.09 ✓ beginning of a sentence
☐ every third word
✓ titles of books and poems
☐ yesterday
✓ names for God

4.010 Teacher check

LIFEPAC TEST

1.–5. Teacher check
6. fences
7. long
8. short
9. name mice use
10. speech float
11. Answers will vary.
12. Answers will vary.
13. before
come
tale
week
yesterday
14. Jeff wanted to surprise his brother John.
Mother was proud of Jeff.
15. burst, struggled, anxious

ALTERNATE LIFEPAC TEST

1.–5. Teacher check
6. tap, cat
7. paid, dine, bead
8. God and names for God
9. beginning of a sentence
10. titles of books
11. holidays and special days
12. alphabetical order:
chair
jump
motor
pool
swing
13. Teacher check handwriting:
Susan loves God. She reads her Bible
everyday. Susan learns more about God
on Sunday.
14. Jeff thought about others.
Tommy was very greedy.
15. Example:
I am the Lord Thy God which have brought
thee out of the land of Egypt.
16. dangerous
17. sobbed
18. worried

SPELLING TEST

1	he	**He** is the tallest boy in our class.	he
2	capital	Begin every sentence with a **capital** letter.	capital
3	cursive	We are learning **cursive** handwriting.	cursive
4	title	The story did not have a **title**.	title
5	only	We were **only** five minutes late.	only
6	two	We get **two** days off every week.	two
7	why	They wanted to know **why** we were late.	why
8	comfort	They live in **comfort** in that large house.	comfort
9	holiday	Is Christmas your favorite **holiday**?	holiday
10	bite	Did a mosquito **bite** you?	bite
11	cape	The queen wore a long **cape**.	cape
12	cute	The puppy is very **cute**.	cute
13	fade	Some colors **fade** in the sun.	fade
14	kite	I fly my **kite** on windy days.	kite
15	use	My sister let me **use** her typewriter.	use
16	copy	Did you **copy** the sentences off the board?	copy
17	long	It is a **long** time until summer vacation.	long
18	beach	We spent our summer at the **beach**.	beach
19	cheer	Did you **cheer** when your team won?	cheer
20	float	That raft will not **float**.	float
21	maid	We hired a **maid** to clean our house.	maid
22	paid	Do you get **paid** for mowing the lawn?	paid
23	speak	You should not **speak** to strangers.	speak
24	activity	Painting is her favorite **activity**.	activity
25	alphabet	We learned the **alphabet** in kindergarten.	alphabet

LANGUAGE ARTS 302

ALTERNATE LIFEPAC TEST

NAME _____

DATE _____

SCORE _____

Each answer = 1 point

Draw a line from the capital printed letter to the capital cursive letter that it matches.

1. O

2. Z

3. G

4. J

5. M

$\mathcal{J}$

$\mathcal{O}$

$\mathcal{M}$

$\mathcal{Z}$

$\mathcal{G}$

Circle the words in which the vowel cannot say its name.

6. go   tap   be   me   cat

Circle the words in which the vowel can say its name.

7. paid   got   dine   bead   pet

Match these words with why they have a capital letter.

8. God   ●   titles of books

9. We are going.   ●   holidays and special days

10. *Pedro and His Bike* ●   beginning of a sentence

11. Labor Day   ●   God and names for God

Put the list below in alphabetical order.

12. jump   _____

       pool   _____

       swing   _____

       chair   _____

       motor   _____

Write the sentences below correctly on the lines.

13. susan loves god. she reads her bible everyday. susan learns more about god on Sunday.

_____

_____

_____

_____

_____

_____

_____

Put a check beside the sentences that tell about *Jeff Learns about Sharing.*

14. _____ Jeff thought about others.

       _____ Tommy was very greedy.

       _____ John went to school.

On the space below, write a sentence that uses capital letters correctly in three different places.

15. _____

_____

Read the words below. Write them correctly in the sentences.

sobbed   dangerous   worried

16. The wind and waves made the lake very

_____ .

17. Scott _____ because he had lost his ball.

18. Mr. Smith was _____ about the fire.

ALTERNATE SPELLING TEST

1	be	I hope you plan to **be** here early.	be
2	correctly	Did you spell all the words **correctly**?	correctly
3	symbol	The flag is a **symbol** of our country.	symbol
4	are	Where **are** you going?	are
5	to	We went **to** a ball game last night.	to
6	your	What is **your** favorite book?	your
7	who	Please tell us **who** you were with.	who
8	connect	Did you **connect** the hose to the faucet?	connect
9	too	We are going **too**.	too
10	section	Which **section** of the newspaper do you enjoy most?	section
11	came	My dog **came** when I called.	came
12	cone	Did you enjoy the ice cream **cone**?	cone
13	dine	We often **dine** at that restaurant.	dine
14	vowel	Can a consonant ever be a **vowel**?	vowel
15	fine	Susan does very **fine** work.	fine
16	short	My little brother is too **short** to reach the cookies.	short
17	pine	Many **pine** trees grow in the forest.	pine
18	bead	One **bead** was missing from the necklace.	bead
19	clean	Our clothes were **clean** after we washed them.	clean
20	goat	My uncle has a **goat** and two sheep on his farm.	goat
21	neat	My room looked **neat** after I picked up the toys.	neat
22	seed	The plant grew from a **seed**.	seed
23	speech	Robert gave a **speech** at our last program.	speech
24	practice	Does your team **practice** everyday?	practice
25	circle	Draw a **circle** around the right answer.	circle

LANGUAGE ARTS 303

Unit 3: Words: Getting to the Roots

TEACHER NOTES

MATERIALS NEEDED FOR LIFEPAC	
Required	Suggested
None	• tagboard • crayons or paint • old magazines • paste • dictionary • newsprint

ADDITIONAL LEARNING ACTIVITIES

Section 1: Dictionary Skills

1. Let students draw different letters of the alphabet on large pieces of tagboard and color them. Pronounce a word from the spelling list. Let students scramble to spell it correctly, standing in places designated for Letter 1, 2, 3, 4, and so on. Repeated letters can be checked by student when the word is spelled.

2. Let students add imaginary words to their own dictionary.

3. Let students begin their own dictionary using words they find difficult to spell, pronounce, or define.

4. Help students pretend they live in a country where they are forbidden to worship God. They must communicate by code, as in example: J̲   BN   HPJOH   UP   UIF   DIVSDI   UP   XPSTIJQ   UIF   M̲PSE. (Hint: Use J for I and B for A.) Answer: I am going to the church to worship the Lord. (Capital letters underlined.)

5. Copy in cursive the entire verse from Psalm 18:30.

Section 2: Prefixes and Suffixes

1. Make tagboard cards of the suffixes and prefixes studied. Give a card to a student until all nine are distributed. Let other students call out root words and write them on the board. Students with the suffix or prefix cards will move move to the proper place (holding the card either in front of or behind the root word) to create the new word.

2. Make a list of words. Plan to exchange with another student for completion of antonyms when other work is done.

3. Let students make their own mini puzzle with boxes and arrows similar to the spelling exercise in this section.

Section 3: Antonyms

1. Write a summary of the story of Button.

2. Write a paragraph explaining what a shepherd does to care for his sheep. Draw a picture illustrating the paragraph.

3. Learn Psalm 23.

Section 4: Synonyms

1. Make list of words. Plan to exchange with other students for completion with synonyms when other work is done.

2. Find pictures of wild animals in magazines. Cut them out and paste them on pieces of construction paper. Make up pet names for each. Write the name under the picture.

3. Using your best handwriting, write the story of David and Goliath (1 Samuel 17:19–49).

Administer the LIFEPAC Spelling Test.

The test is provided in this Teacher's Guide.
Evaluate the tests and review the words the students spelled incorrectly.
If necessary, review all of the words in the unit to prepare for the alternate spelling test.
Administer the Alternate LIFEPAC Spelling test that is provided in this Teacher's Guide.

Administer the LIFEPAC Test.

The test is to be administered in one session. Give no help except with directions.
Evaluate the tests and review areas where the students have done poorly.
Review the pages and activities that stress the concepts tested.
If necessary, administer the Alternate LIFEPAC Test.

ANSWER KEYS

SECTION 1

1.1 Jacky, Janet, Jean, Jill, Joyce
1.2 page 89
1.3 cat, cave
1.4 Example: catsup, caught
1.5 prince, basket, throw
1.6 Answers will vary.
1.7 Teacher check
1.8 chief
1.9 no
1.10 Example: The waves softly lapped against his dinghy.
1.11 Either order:
  a. A stout wooden stick to hit a ball in baseball.
  b. A flying mammal that flies by radar.
1.12 Teacher check
1.13 Teacher check
1.14 heard, silly, bird, curl, circle, dog, perch, tree
1.15 herd   —   a group of animals
  jerk   —   a sudden pull
  burst   —   break open
  nurse   —   a person who cares for sick people
1.16 Examples:
  I like to play in the dirt.
  Mother is always in a hurry.
  I hope to have a new curtain for the window.
1.17 perfect
1.18 Answers will vary.
1.19 heard, herd
1.20 Teacher check

SELF TEST 1

1.01 God
1.02 dictionary
1.03 entry word
1.04 alphabetical order
1.05 guide words
1.06–1.08 Answers will vary.
1.09 ✓ how to pronounce words
  ☐ how to read
  ✓ how to spell words
  ✓ what words mean
  ☐ how to swim
  ☐ things you need for a trip
1.010 dirt
1.011 word
1.012 curl
1.013 Teacher check

SECTION 2

2.1–2.4 Answers will vary.
2.5 uncommon, unclear, unpaid
2.6 redo, rebuild, reheat
2.7 redo
2.8 rebuild
2.9 reheat
2.10 not true
2.11 not believable
2.12 unload, unfold, unpack
2.13 unload
2.14 unfolded
2.15 unpacked
2.16 cooling, cooled, cools, combing, combed, combs
2.17 helps, helped, helping, kicks, kicked, kicking
2.18 growled
2.19 growling
2.20 growls
2.21 lovely, slowly, smoothly
2.22 friendly, godly
2.23 godly, friendly
2.24 farmer, teacher, hunter
2.25 painter, singer
2.26 singer, painter
2.27 thankful, careful, wishful
2.28 truthful, useful
2.29 useful, truthful
2.30 unthankful, untruthful
2.31 un—not
untruthful—not truthful
truthful—full of truth
ful—full of or enough to fill
unthankful—not thankful
thankful—full of thanks
2.32 unorderly, unthankful, redoing
2.33 guard, park
2.34 Answers will vary.
2.35 1. march
2. harm
3. alarm
2.36 Example:
Many ships were anchored in the harbor.
2.37 smart, sharp, cartoon
2.38 heart
2.39 Teacher check

SELF TEST 2

2.01–2.03 Answers will vary.
2.04 (curl) (word) (circle)
2.05 car
2.06 Teacher check
2.07 Teacher check
2.08 (true) (lone) (use) (build) (skill)
2.09 beginning
2.010 end
2.011 not, the opposite of
2.012 full of, enough to fill
2.013 suffixes
2.014 prays, prayed, praying
Answers will vary.
2.015 unsafe
2.016 swiftly
2.017 climber
2.018 climbs
2.019 joyful
2.020 basketful, kindly, restudy camper, untrue

SECTION 3

3.1 Answers will vary.
Yes
3.2 Answers will vary.
3.3 Days and months
3.4 We show our love to others on Valentine's Day in February. In December, we celebrate God's love in sending Jesus. Christians can celebrate God's love from January to December and Sunday through Saturday, because we have God's love in our hearts.
3.5 exactly opposite of
3.6 cold
3.7 healthy
3.8 poor
3.9 wild
3.10 hard-easy   strong-weak
clean-dirty   sweet-sour
3.11 Answers will vary.
3.12–3.14 Teacher check
3.15 Tuesday, Wednesday, Thursday, Friday, Saturday, Sunday
3.16 Monday
3.17 February, September, October, December
3.18 January, March, April, May, June, July, August, November
3.19 Teacher check
3.20 2, 4, 1, 6, 3, 5, 8, 7
3.21 butterfly
3.22 adventure
3.23 wiggled
3.24 born
3.25 flock
3.26 pasture
3.27 sheepfold
3.28 staff
3.29 enemy
3.30 content
3.31 wandered
3.32 mischief
3.33 scars
3.34 gently
3.35 tenderly
3.36 Answers will vary.

SELF TEST 3

3.01 Teacher check
3.02 Answers will vary.
3.03–3.04 Either order: unhappy, bowlful
3.05 sad, sail, sale, same, sand
3.06–3.07 Examples:
bō a curved shape like a rainbow
bou to bend the head or body showing respect
3.08 the opposite
3.09 ✓ up/down
☐ sunny/bright
✓ low/high
✓ day/night
☐ big/large
☐ glad/happy
3.010 afternoon   —   morning
asleep   —   awake
beautiful   —   ugly
buy   —   sell
broken   —   fixed
plain   —   fancy
hate   —   love
3.011 1, 3, 5, 4, 2

SECTION 4

4.1	Mr.Baker
4.2	Mrs. Baker
4.3	Miss Walker
4.4	Dr. Farmer
4.5	Rev. Brown
4.6	Miss Smith
4.7	Miss Mary March
4.8	Mr. Hal Howe
4.9	Rev. Max Miller
4.10	Answers will vary.
4.11	the same
4.12	jolly
4.13	big
4.14	ill
4.15	Answers will vary.
4.16	talk/speak
	jump/hop
	mean/cruel
4.17	fourth, pour, poor
4.18	Teacher check
4.19	forget, north
4.20	torn, shore
4.21	Answers will vary.
4.22	to come forward
4.23	Example: The boy stepped forth.
4.24	the one after third
4.25	Example: I am in the fourth grade.
4.26	Examples:
	A little hole in the skin is a pore.
	I will pour a glass of milk.
	I am a poor speller.
4.27	Lord
4.28	order
4.29	report
4.30	force
4.31	Example: The porcupine has sharp spines.
4.32–4.35	Teacher check
4.36	Answers will vary.
4.37	Teacher check

SELF TEST 4

4.01	un(thankful) basket(ful) (read)er (re)wind tender(ly)
4.02	helpful
4.03	friendly
4.04	reopen
4.05	unkind
4.06	untie
4.07	reader
4.08	names of people
	days of the week
	months
	God and names for God
	titles of books and poems
	names of pets
	countries, states, and cities
	holidays and special days
	titles in people's names
4.09	Dr. Lamb gave Mrs. Peters a pet bird named Oscar.
4.010	Teacher check
4.011	no
4.012	dirt torn north poor forth march heart
4.013	✓ beautiful/pretty
	☐ poor/rich
	✓ happy/jolly
	☐ good/bad
	☐ mad/happy
	✓ talk/speak
4.014	✓ empty/full
	✓ strong/weak
	✓ cold/hot
	☐ big/large
	☐ nice/kind
	✓ hate/love
4.015	forth
4.016	poor
4.017	fourth
4.018	pour
4.019	pore

LIFEPAC TEST

1. ✓ meaning of words
   ☐ how to make words
   ✓ how to pronounce words
   ✓ how to spell words
   ☐ how to write stories
2. ✓ inside, outside, over, under, wonderful
   ☐ camera, before, yesterday, coming, typing
   ✓ sandwich, scamper, scary, scatter, scold
   ☐ repair, ribbon, roast, rubber, rose
3. Answers will vary.
4. helps a doctor   — nurse
   a round shape   — circle
   a group of animals — herd
   a place to shop   — market
   a name for God   — Lord
5. helps   helper
   helping   helpful
   helped   unhelpful
6. synonyms—meaning the same
   guide words—help you find words in the dictionary
   alphabetical order—in the order of the alphabet
   entry word—each word in a dictionary
   antonyms—opposite in meaning
7. yesterday   — today
   awake   — asleep
   plain   — fancy
   broken   — fixed
   borrow   — return
8. jump   — leap
   small   — little
   home   — house
   happy   — glad
   giggle   — laugh
9. sheepfold
10. pasture
11. staff
12. born
13. wiggles
14. content
15. tenderly

ALTERNATE LIFEPAC TEST

1. Teacher check
2. spelling
   each word's meaning
   words in alphabetical order
   how to use words in sentences
   guide words to help us find words
3. happy
   merry
4. good
   heart
   joy
   my
   run
5. small—big
   hop—sit
   cool—hot
6. names of days
7. names of pets
8. countries, states, cities
9. names of months
10. titles of books and poems
11. names of holidays
12. titles in person's name
13. people's names
14. 3
    4
    2
    1
15. Examples:
    unthankful   thankful
    thanks   thanked
    thanking
16. fort
    market
    bird
    curl
    fern
    horse
    morning
17. Teacher check
    Example: Fido came when Jerry called him.

SPELLING TEST

1	born	Joe was **born** in Arizona.	born
2	poor	They gave food to the **poor** family.	poor
3	plain	The choir wore **plain** robes.	plain
4	circle	The children made a **circle** in the snow.	circle
5	word	The **word** in the lesson was spelled correctly.	word
6	north	Canada is **north** of the United States.	north
7	report	The girl had to **report** on her summer vacation.	report
8	asleep	Grandmother was **asleep** when I called.	asleep
9	fancy	All the bands had **fancy** uniforms.	fancy
10	market	The food **market** was two miles away.	market
11	heart	Jesus will come into your **heart** if you ask Him.	heart
12	alarm	Father always set his **alarm** clock.	alarm
13	cartoon	The book had a **cartoon** on its cover.	cartoon
14	herd	A large **herd** of cattle was on Uncle Harry's farm.	herd
15	curl	Our dog loves to **curl** up by the fireplace.	curl
16	burst	Jane **burst** the balloon with a pin.	burst
17	force	A police **force** is needed in every city.	force
18	save	The fireman tried to **save** the burning building.	save
19	love	Jesus told about the **love** of God.	love
20	guard	Their dog was a good **guard** at night.	guard
21	nurse	Jane's sister is a **nurse** at the hospital.	nurse
22	perfect	The story had a **perfect** ending.	perfect
23	shore	Children played on the **shore** of the ocean.	shore
24	porcupine	A young **porcupine** was born in the zoo.	porcupine
25	morning	John woke up early in the **morning**.	morning

LANGUAGE ARTS 303

ALTERNATE LIFEPAC TEST

NAME _____

DATE _____

SCORE _____

40 / 50

Each answer = 1 point

Write a word for each capital letter below. Be sure to join when you should.

1.

Check what a dictionary tells us.

2. _____ spelling

_____ each word's meaning

_____ words in alphabetical order

_____ how to write numbers

_____ how to read

_____ how to use words in sentences

_____ guide words to help us find words

Circle the synonyms for *jolly*.

3. happy   sad   good   merry

Write this list of words in alphabetical order.

4. joy   _____

good   _____

my   _____

heart   _____

run   _____

Put an *X* in the box if the word pairs are antonyms.

5. ☐ small—big   ☐ hop—sit   ☐ cool—hot
    ☐ jumped—leaped   ☐ laugh—giggle   ☐ home—house

Match the words to why they are capitalized.

6. Monday   ●   names of pets
7. Buster   ●   title in person's name
8. Canada   ●   titles of books and poems
9. June   ●   names of days
10. *The Lost Lamb* ●   names of months
11. Valentine's Day ●   names of holidays or special days
12. Mr. Davis   ●   countries, states, cities
13. Susan   ●   people's names

Number the sentences below in the order they happened in the story about *Button, the Lamb*.

14. _____ The shepherd said, "I am the door."

_____ Button got lost.

_____ The shepherd killed the lion.

_____ Button was born.

Make five new words using the prefix and the suffixes with the root word *thank*.

15. un-   -s   -ing   -ed   -ful

_____

_____

_____

_____

_____

Circle the words that have an *r*-**controlled vowel.**

16. run   fort   brake   market   bird   curl
       ferm   rope   horse   morning   bright   print

Write a sentence that uses your pet's name or the name of a friend's pet. Use capital letters correctly.

17. _____

_____

_____

_____

_____

ALTERNATE SPELLING TEST

1	broken	Only one store would repair **broken** toys.	broken
2	afternoon	By late **afternoon**, the rain ended.	afternoon
3	harm	The trainer said no **harm** would come to the animal.	harm
4	perch	An owl liked to **perch** on the branch.	perch
5	heard	All the students **heard** the siren.	heard
6	jerk	It took a big **jerk** to free the fishing line.	jerk
7	quarrel	Did the teams **quarrel** about the ball game?	quarrel
8	farmer	Bob's dad is a **farmer**.	farmer
9	pour	I will **pour** the water into the glasses.	pour
10	order	The teacher gave the **order** to stand up.	order
11	torn	Tom repaired the **torn** page in his book.	torn
12	Lord	The **Lord** Jesus wants to be in your life.	Lord
13	borrow	Betty asked to **borrow** Susan's pencil.	borrow
14	fixed	Uncle Joe **fixed** the broken wheel.	fixed
15	awake	The rooster is **awake** early in the morning.	awake
16	harbor	The sailing ships came into the **harbor**.	harbor
17	march	The band would always **march** after the game.	march
18	hurry	The team had to **hurry** out to the field.	hurry
19	sharp	Watch out for the **sharp** corners.	sharp
20	apart	Janet took the toy car **apart**.	apart
21	hate	The Bible says you should love and not **hate**.	hate
22	beautiful	The children saw a **beautiful** mountain.	beautiful
23	park	Did the bus driver **park** the school bus?	park
24	fourth	The **fourth** boy in line is Frank.	fourth
25	cart	On the farm they had a **cart** and a pony.	cart

LANGUAGE ARTS 304

Unit 4: Words: How to Use Them

TEACHER NOTES

MATERIALS NEEDED FOR LIFEPAC	
Required	Suggested
None	• drawing paper (12- x 18-inch sheets) • pencils • crayons • glue • heavy cardboard • dry vegetables (beans, peas, etc.) or pasta in various shapes

ADDITIONAL LEARNING ACTIVITIES

Section 1: Nouns and Adjectives

1. Prepare a book of riddles (both original and circulating) for exchange.

2. Make a large circle and divide it into pie-shaped wedges. Color each wedge. Cut out wheel. Attach to back support so that it can be swung. Make a list of words and then add adjectives from the color wheel (*hippopotamus—yellow, purple,* or *pink,* etc.).

3. From the spelling list, make list of rhyming words.

Section 2: Verbs and Adverbs

1. Write a sentence. Draw a picture to illustrate it.

2. Write directions to

   a. cook an egg,

   b. walk to the door of the classroom,

   c. hammer a nail,

   d. make a friend,

   e. help Dad plant the garden, or

   f. find a passage in the Bible.

3. Continue the story of Noah (Genesis 7:11–8:12).

Section 3: Punctuation Marks

1. Allow time for students to play more games of Silly Sentences.

2. Fill small containers with dried beans (pinto, lima, butter, navy, etc.) or pasta of various shapes and sizes. Label each container with a part of speech (noun, verb, adjective, etc.). Have students write a simple sentence on a small piece of heavy cardboard. Exchange sentences. Have students label each part of speech below the words in the sentence. Then, students should glue the correct bean or pasta below the part of speech it represents. If desired, students can draw pictures illustrating their sentences and color them.

3. Let students take turns going back and forth to the door in a variety of ways (hop, skip, walk backwards, crawl, etc.) and ask other students to write a sentence describing the gait.

Section 4: Two Meanings

1. Copy the proper nouns from the story of Joshua commanding the sun to stand still (Joshua 10:1–15).

2. Write a paragraph about Zacchaeus wanting to see Jesus (Luke 19:1–10).

Administer the LIFEPAC Spelling Test.

The test is provided in this Teacher's Guide.
Evaluate the tests and review the words the students spelled incorrectly.
If necessary, review all of the words in the unit to prepare for the alternate spelling test.
Administer the Alternate LIFEPAC Spelling test that is provided in this Teacher's Guide.

Administer the LIFEPAC Test.

The test is to be administered in one session. Give no help except with directions.
Evaluate the tests and review areas where the students have done poorly.
Review the pages and activities that stress the concepts tested.
If necessary, administer the Alternate LIFEPAC Test.

ANSWER KEYS

SECTION 1

1.1 Examples: language, words, section
1.2 Examples: big, little, red
1.3 (nail) (candy) (pastor) (inventor) (bicycle,) (museum,) (whale,) (potato)
1.4 baker
1.5 island
1.6 pencil
1.7

Person	Place	Thing
sailor	village	radio
cousin	church	banana
queen	neighborhood	bear

1.8 places to learn
1.9 people in family
1.10 places to learn
1.11 things to eat
1.12 animals
1.13 people in family
1.14 things to eat
1.15 animals
1.16–1.25 Examples:
monkey
dog
city
airplane
rose
country
brother
pencil
church
pear
1.26 Examples:

tall, thin	hot, yummy
spooky, old	soft, black

1.27 (six) (twenty) (many) (three)
this those that ten
(several) (some) these (fourteen)
1.28

✓ beautiful	✓ greedy
☐ apple	✓ long
✓ warm	✓ red
☐ girls	✓ smooth
☐ bird	☐ playground
✓ ripe	☐ road

1.29–1.38 Examples:
big
pretty, yellow
beautiful, blue
tired, old
happy
cold
many
sick, little
nine
huge, gray
1.39 Teacher check
1.40 Teacher check
1.41 Teacher check
1.42 neighborhood
1.43 hook
1.44 shoulder
1.45 rooster
1.46 treasure
1.47 spoil
1.48 fool
1.49 broom
1.50 famous
1.51 measure
1.52 touch
1.53 join
1.54 surround
1.55 already
1.56 taught
1.57 Any order: broom, fool, rooster
1.58 Any order: hook, neighborhood
1.59 Any order: already, treasure, measure
1.60 yes
1.61 Any order: join, spoil
1.62 shoulder
1.63 famous
1.64 surround
1.65 taught
1.66 Teacher check
1.67 Teacher check
1.68 Answers will vary.

SELF TEST 1

1.01 noun
1.02 adjective
1.03 ✓ person
        ✓ place
        ☐ verbs
        ✓ things
        ✓ animals
1.04 ✓ teacher   ☐ happy
        ✓ fruit   ☐ go
        ☐ crawl   ✓ house
        ✓ keys   ✓ lion
1.05 ⬭green, soft, fat, round, many, sweet
1.06–1.11 Examples:
        farmer
        church
        dog
        black
        pink
        many
1.012 ⬭treasure, hook, spoil, touch, fool
1.013 Teacher check

SECTION 2

2.1 Examples: learned, tells, are going
2.2 Examples: hard, fast, quietly
2.3 hit
2.4–2.9 Examples:
        climbed
        ran
        jumped
        eats
        hit
        drops
2.10 ⬭spill kick ride chop break crawl
2.11 was or is
2.12 were or are
2.13 was or is
2.14 were or are
2.15 Joan <u>poured</u> a glass of water.
2.16 Kate's dog <u>barks</u> at strangers.
2.17 Mice <u>nibble</u> cheese.
2.18 Jesus <u>loves</u> you.
2.19 The ship <u>sailed</u> yesterday.
2.20–2.24 Examples:
2.20 played
2.21 is
2.22 jumped
2.23 cut
2.24 prayed
2.25 Janet sings <u>beautifully</u>.
2.26 Doug skates <u>fast</u>.
2.27 His sister ran <u>quietly</u>.
2.28 The boy will run <u>tomorrow</u>.
2.29 Terry walked <u>yesterday</u>.
2.30 Grandma visits <u>tonight</u>.
2.31 The little boy lives <u>here</u>.
2.32 Monica played <u>inside</u>.
2.33 Joshua marched <u>outside</u>.
2.34 how, when, where, verbs
2.35–2.43 Examples:
        peacefully
        bravely
        inside
        softly
        angrily
        yesterday
        nicely
        happily
        there
2.44 Teacher check
2.45 Teacher check

2.46	allow	growl	plow
	frown	howl	
2.47	below	narrow	grown
	fellow	pillow	thrown
2.48	stew		
2.49	view		
2.50	draw, drawer		
2.51	draw		
2.52	drawer		
2.53	allow		
2.54	bellow		
2.55	narrow		
2.56	howl		
2.57	growl		
2.58	fellow		
2.59	frown		
2.60	grown		
2.61	thrown		
2.62	pillow		
2.63	plow		
2.64	stew		
2.65	view		

2.66–2.69 Teacher check
2.70 a clown
2.71 Teacher check
2.72 a cat
2.73 Teacher check

SELF TEST 2

2.01 noun
2.02 adjective
2.03 verb
2.04 adverb
2.05 ball friend house candy bear
2.06 blue
2.07 big black
2.08 kind little
2.09 is
2.010 scampered
2.011 sweeps
2.012 sings
2.013 melted
2.014 ate
2.015 wrote
2.016 where when how
2.017 carefully
2.018 quickly
2.019 here
2.020 stew drawer plow
2.021 taught hook neighbor
2.022 Teacher check
2.023 a snowman

SECTION 3

3.1 ?
3.2 .
3.3 .
3.4 ?
3.5 ?
3.6 .
3.7 !
3.8 ?
3.9 !
3.10 ?
3.11 .
3.12 !
3.13 .
3.14 !
3.15 !
3.16 Teacher check
3.17 Next Wednesday is my birthday.
3.18 My favorite teacher, Mr. John Taylor, is from Australia.
3.19 Watch out, Peggy!
3.20 We celebrate Christmas for Jesus' birthday.
3.21 My pet bird, Perky, was hatched in August.
3.22 "The Lord gave us the Bible for our guidebook," said Rev. Jenkins.
3.23 second
3.24 The nice   farmer   cried   quietly.
3.25 The little   boy   skipped   happily.
3.26 The large   buffalo   ran   easily.
3.27 The cute   children   scampered   down.
3.28 Answers will vary.
3.29 Answers will vary.
3.30 build
3.31 bild
3.32 make by putting material together
3.33 verb
3.34 adj.
3.35 n. adj.
3.36 adj. adv.
3.37 n. v.
3.38 Teacher check
3.39 Teacher check
3.40 Teacher check

SELF TEST 3

3.01 ?
3.02 .
3.03 !
3.04 ?
3.05 .
3.06 !
3.07–3.015 Teacher check
3.016 name a person, place, or thing
3.017 tell what someone is doing
3.018 tell about a noun
3.019 tell about a verb
3.020 Example: The nice girl works hard.
3.021 ✓ spelling
       ✓ meaning
       ☐ how to build
       ✓ kinds of words
       ☐ time of day
       ✓ pronunciation
3.022 Teacher check

SECTION 4

4.1	wee—small	
	mean—cruel	
	talk—speak	
4.2	day—night	
	full—empty	
	truth—lie	
	<u>synonym</u>	<u>antonym</u>
4.3	happy	sad
4.4	good	bad
4.5	wealthy	poor
4.6	reload, redo, undo, unload, unfold, rebuild	
	helpful, thankful, friendly, helper, camper	
4.7	helps	
4.8	helping	
4.9	helped	
4.10	redo	
4.11	undo	
4.12	Teacher check	
4.13	Teacher check	
4.14	bicycle syllable	
4.15	every candy body	
4.16	doorway chimney yesterday daydream	
	valley turkey donkey	
4.17	obey	
4.18	lying	
4.19	bicycle, candy, chimney, daydream, donkey	
4.20	doorway, enjoy, everybody, lying, obey	
4.21	royal, syllable, turkey, valley, yesterday	
4.22–4.27	Teacher check	
4.28	camels	
4.29	caves	
4.30	to help them	
4.31	I will help you	
4.32	a poor farmer	
4.33	a fleece	
4.34	32,000	
4.35	afraid	
4.36	300	
4.37	God's plan	
4.38	blew trumpets, smashed pitchers, and shouted	
4.39	God won	
4.40	You can always trust God to help you	
4.41	Teacher check	

SELF TEST 4

4.01	beginning	
4.02	end	
4.03	truth fold read friend walk	
4.04	a similar meaning	
4.05	opposite meaning	
4.06	☐ sweet—sour	
	☐ hot—cold	
	✓ pop—burst	
	✓ nice—kind	
4.07	✓ low—high	
	☐ pretty—lovely	
	☐ talk—speak	
	✓ hard—easy	
4.08	smoother	
4.09	unhappy	
4.010	climber	
4.011	cupful	
4.012	reopen	
4.013	bicycle candy enjoy	
4.014	✓ ball	
	bat	
	boat	
	bump	

4.015			
Gideon	—	b.	a poor farmer
Israelites	—	c.	God's people
300 men	—	e.	surrounded the Midianites
fleece	—	f.	test God
Midianites	—	d.	fought each other and ran
God	—	a.	won against Midianites

LIFEPAC TEST

1. verb
2. adjective
3. adverb
4. noun
5. Example: The cute monkey climbed quickly.
6. (taught) (hook) (measure)
7. (allow) (narrow) (view)
8. Teacher check
9. a smiling face
10. !
11. ?
12. .
13. !
14. Don moved to Newport from Great Falls. He likes his new teacher, Mr. Fisher. Don's birthday is on Valentine's Day, February 14. Don has a pet dog called Spot.
15. build—spelling
    (bild)—pronunciation make by putting together—meaning
    v.—kind of word
16. (farmer)
17. (fleece)
18. (afraid)
19. tiny—wee
    evil—bad
20. hot—cold
    good—bad
    tame—wild
21. builder or rebuild
22. teacher or reteach
23. quickly or quicker
24. cupful
25. redo or undo
26. (obey) (lying) (donkey)
27. Teacher check

ALTERNATE LIFEPAC TEST

1. name of a person, place, thing, or animal
2. words with similar meanings
3. action word
4. describes verbs
5. words opposite in meanings
6. add to the beginning of a root word
7. describes nouns
8. add to end of a root word
9. wee—small
   giant—big
   pretty—beautiful
10. night—day
    little—big
    hot—cold
    slow—fast
11. basketful
    slowly
    singer
    remake
    unload
12. syllable, turkey, bicycle
13. Gideon was a farmer.
    God's plan won.
    Three hundred men surprised the Midianites.
14. meanings, spellings, how to pronounce a word, parts of a sentence
15.–24. Teacher check; examples:
15. Today is Friday.
16. Mr. Jones came home.
17. God our Father created the earth.
18. Mary, Tom, and Jane left for school.
19. *The Skies Will Hold Them* is my favorite book.
20. Easter comes on April 15th this year.
21. My hometown is New York City.
22. Come here, Fido.
23. Tuesday, July 11, 2016, was a hot day.
24. Dr. Smith delivered the sermon.
25. !
26. ?
27. .
28. Example:
    The blue car sped quickly down the street.
29. plow, stew, howl
30. shoulder, measure
31. Teacher check
32. Teacher check

SPELLING TEST

1	broom	Use the **broom** to sweep the floor.	broom
2	taught	She **taught** me how to subtract numbers.	taught
3	hook	He put the fish bait on the **hook**.	hook
4	surround	Trees **surround** my house.	surround
5	measure	**Measure** the flour carefully.	measure
6	neighborhood	I live in a nice **neighborhood**.	neighborhood
7	touch	Don't **touch** the hot stove!	touch
8	spoil	If you eat a snack now, you will **spoil** your dinner.	spoil
9	already	They left for church **already**.	already
10	allow	Father will not **allow** me to go.	allow
11	draw	Will you **draw** a picture for me?	draw
12	fellow	He's a friendly **fellow**.	fellow
13	growl	The dog will **growl** if you go near it.	growl
14	grown	He has **grown** three inches in two months.	grown
15	narrow	**Narrow** is the way to heaven.	narrow
16	plow	The farmer will **plow** his fields next week.	plow
17	stew	We had **stew** for dinner.	stew
18	bicycle	She rides a **bicycle** to school.	bicycle
19	donkey	Mary rode a **donkey** to Bethlehem.	donkey
20	obey	Children, **obey** your parents.	obey
21	valley	Our city is in a **valley**.	valley
22	candy	Are you allowed to eat **candy**?	candy
23	enjoy	Do you **enjoy** sewing?	enjoy
24	royal	Purple is a **royal** color.	royal
25	yesterday	**Yesterday** was my birthday.	yesterday

LANGUAGE ARTS 304

ALTERNATE LIFEPAC TEST

NAME _____

DATE _____

SCORE _____

40

50

Each answer = 1 point

Match the words to the correct answer.

1. noun • action word
2. synonym • words opposite in meanings
3. verb • name of a person, place, thing, or animal
4. adverb • add to end of a root word
5. antonym • words with similar meanings
6. prefix • add to the beginning of a root word
7. adjective • describes verbs
8. suffix • describes nouns

Check the word pairs that are synonyms.

9. ☐ on—under   ☐ funny—sad   ☐ wee—small
   ☐ giant—big   ☐ pretty—beautiful   ☐ run—walk

Check the word pairs that are antonyms.

10. ☐ night—day   ☐ little—big   ☐ make—do
    ☐ hot—cold   ☐ sing—hum   ☐ slow—fast

Make new words using the prefixes, suffixes, and root words below.

11. -er   -ly   -ful   un-   re-

basket   _____

slow   _____

sing   _____

make   _____

load   _____

Circle the spelling words with _y_ as a vowel.

12.   yo yo   syllable   yawn   turkey   bicycle

Put an _X_ in the box if the sentence is true about Gideon.

13.   ☐ Gideon was a farmer.

☐ The Israelites invited the Midianites to live in their land.

☐ Gideon took 32,000 men to defeat the enemy.

☐ God's plan won.

☐ hree hundred men surprised the Midianites.

Put an _X_ in the box if it tells what a dictionary tells.

14.   ☐ meanings   ☐ how to read
          ☐ how to write   ☐ how to pronounce a word
          ☐ spellings   ☐ parts of a sentence

Write an example for each capital rule.

15.   beginning of a sentence

_____

_____

_____

_____

16.   title in a person's name

_____
- -
_____
_____
- -
_____

17.   God and names for God

_____
- -
_____
_____
- -
_____

18.   people's names

_____
- -
_____
_____
- -
_____

19.   titles of books and poems

_____
- -
_____
_____
- -
_____

20.   holidays and special days

_____
- -
_____
_____
- -
_____

21. countries, states, and cities

_____
- -
_____

22. names of pets

_____
- -
_____
- -
_____

23. names of days and months

_____
- -
_____
_____
- -
_____

24. Mr., Mrs., Ms., Miss, Dr., and Rev.

_____
- -
_____
_____
- -
_____

Match the correct punctuation to its use.

25.	strong feeling, surprise	●	?
26.	asks a question	●	.
27.	tells us something	●	!

Write a sentence that uses a noun, adjective, adverb, and verb.

28.
- -
_____
_____
- -
_____

Circle the spelling words that have a *w*-controlled vowel.

29. way   plow   will   stew   howl

Circle the spelling words with irregular vowel teams.

30. shoulder   meat   goat   measure

Write the following sentence in correct handwriting.

31. We should love one another.

_____

- -

_____

- -

_____

32. Read and follow the directions below.
     a. Find a friend.
     b. Tell this friend your name.
     c. Listen to your friend tell you his or her name.
     d. Say, "You are my friend."
     e. Listen to your friend say, "You are my friend, too."

ALTERNATE SPELLING TEST

1	broom	Use the **broom** to sweep the floor.	broom
2	famous	Abraham Lincoln was a **famous** man.	famous
3	fool	If you **fool** around, you might get hurt.	fool
4	measure	**Measure** the flour carefully.	measure
5	treasure	Did he find the buried **treasure**?	treasure
6	touch	Don't **touch** the hot stove!	touch
7	shoulder	Is your **shoulder** hurt?	shoulder
8	rooster	Our **rooster** crows every morning.	rooster
9	join	We would like to **join** this team.	join
10	below	Look **below** to find the instructions.	below
11	drawer	The **drawer** was left open.	drawer
12	frown	It's better to smile than to **frown**.	frown
13	view	The **view** of the city is beautiful!	view
14	howl	My dog likes to **howl** when I sing.	howl
15	pillow	My **pillow** is big and fluffy.	pillow
16	stew	We had **stew** for dinner.	stew
17	thrown	Who hasn't **thrown** the ball yet?	thrown
18	bicycle	She rides a **bicycle** to school.	bicycle
19	chimney	We have a brick **chimney** on our roof.	chimney
20	everybody	**Everybody** had a good time today.	everybody
21	valley	Our city is in a **valley**.	valley
22	doorway	He had to duck to get through the **doorway**.	doorway
23	daydream	You shouldn't **daydream** in class.	daydream
24	lying	He was **lying** about who broke the window.	lying
25	turkey	Do you eat **turkey** on Thanksgiving Day?	turkey

LANGUAGE ARTS 305

Unit 5: Sentence: Start to Finish

TEACHER NOTES

MATERIALS NEEDED FOR LIFEPAC	
Required	Suggested
None	• manila paper • crayons • finger paint and paper • whistle • tagboard

ADDITIONAL LEARNING ACTIVITIES

Section 1: Nouns and Adjectives

1. Begin a story, stop when whistle blows, let next person in circle pick it up and continue until whistle blows, and so on.

2. Let each child make large (8"x10") tagboard symbols for question marks, periods, commas, and exclamation marks. Let one child take his symbols to use as the person in charge for a game of "Red Light." (No one moves toward the goal line without a command from "it" who uses the signs to control movement without speaking. Anyone moving without command moves to the sidelines; the person getting to the finish line first on commands becomes "it" next time.)

3. Make puzzles of own choosing to share with other groups using names of birds, sports, months of the year or days of the week, or food.

4. Give one sentence for a paragraph. Let students add details.
   Examples: My dad and I went fishing.
   My favorite Bible story is _____ .
   One way to save energy is to watch our use of power in the house.
   God made the birds of the air and the fish of the sea.

5. Make list of items in puzzle from previous activity (Group activity) and alphabetize them.

6. Make a puzzle using names of states.

7. Draw pictures illustrating antonyms: up, down; hot, cold; day, night; and so on.

8. Using finger paints, use capital letters to make a design.

9. Distribute pages from magazines (ads or stories) and ask students to underline vowels.

Section 2: Capitals, Punctuation, and Plurals

1. Discuss these questions with your class.
   a. Why did the man take the little dog to the farm?
   b. What is a better way to get rid of unwanted animals?
   c. What could have happened to the puppy?
   d. What should Kenny have done to be sure that the puppy did not belong to anyone?

2. One student is chosen to be "it." He thinks of a capital letter. Other children, taking turns, ask him questions that can be answered by *yes* or *no*. Questions may concern the shape, sound, or use of the letter in words. Allow only twenty questions before declaring a winner.

3. In pairs, students each make up a list of nouns (birds, animals, household articles, items in classroom, etc.). Exchanging lists, the second student changes the nouns into plurals.

4. Add other vegetables (and words) to word garden to practice the spelling words. Color the vegetables.

5. Write sentences using !'s or ?'s and exchange with other students. Students answer the questions and draw pictures illustrating the exclamatory sentences.

6. Draw a picture of Kenny and Zipper.

7. Copy the Pledge of Allegiance using proper capitalization.

Section 3: Reading and Writing Paragraphs

1. Discuss these questions with your class.

   a. Why did his mother let Kenny keep the puppy?

   b. Who found Zipper when he was lost?

   c. Is there a better place to tie a puppy than a clothesline?

   d. Why did Mrs. Winters want to take Zipper home?

   e. Did Zipper ever get lost again? Why?

2. Let students each make a list of nouns. Ask them to arrange them in columns according to person, place, or thing. Then, ask them to alphabetize them within each column.

3. Write the names of three favorite books in cursive, paying particular attention to the formation of capital letters.

4. Learn Philippians 4:8 by heart and copy it, taking care to place the commas correctly.

5. Draw a picture of Kenny's house.

6. Describe Moses, David, or one of the disciples in a paragraph.

7. Write a paragraph telling how your house looks in the daytime. Then, write a paragraph telling how your house looks at night.

Administer the LIFEPAC Spelling Test.

The test is provided in this Teacher's Guide.
Evaluate the tests and review the words the students spelled incorrectly.
If necessary, review all of the words in the unit to prepare for the alternate spelling test.
Administer the Alternate LIFEPAC Spelling test that is provided in this Teacher's Guide.

Administer the LIFEPAC Test.

The test is to be administered in one session. Give no help except with directions.
Evaluate the tests and review areas where the students have done poorly.
Review the pages and activities that stress the concepts tested.
If necessary, administer the Alternate LIFEPAC Test.

ANSWER KEYS

SECTION 1

1.1 a bird

1.2 half a one-inch circle

1.3 draw them on using a crayon or colored pencil

1.4 There are many animals to see at the zoo.

1.5 learn about the animals.

1.6 a person can get close to animals

1.7 a whale

1.8 a moose

1.9 a giraffe

1.10 an octopus

1.11 Teacher check: Answers will vary.

1.12–1.13

a. <u>Col. 1</u>	b. <u>Col. 2</u>	c. <u>Col. 3</u>
ankle 1	beef 1	correct 1
cake 1	deal 1	grip 1
fright 1	ice 2	heavy 1
join 2	race 3	join 2
pony 2	shopping 3	kick 2
quit 2	voice 3	train 3

1.14

<u>Across</u>	<u>Down</u>
1. hot	2. over
4. inside	3. dark
6. fast	5. near
9. back	7. tall
10. large	8. wet
12. day	9. black
13. work	11. new

1.15–1.19 Answers will vary but should include words from 1.14.

1.20 stepping

1.21 raced

1.22 gloomy

1.23 exclaimed

1.24 dull

1.25 The children went swimming after they finished their chores. Another possible answer is: After they finished their chores, the children went swimming.

1.26 The large bowl was full of ripe fruit.

1.27 happy swing fox net bug

1.28

S	map	L	rude
S	bit	S	lamp
L	rode	S	truck
S	mad	L	pay
L	kind	S	rocks
S	dust	L	made
S	fox	S	rod
L	use	L	side

1.29

a. pat	b. sit
c. but	d. leg
e. beg	

1.30

Wagon	Dog	Potato
2	1	3
2	1	3
Airplane	Man	Bike
2	1	1
2	1	1
Baseball	Tire	Fish
2	1	1
2	1	1

1.31 Sam and Jan (or Jen or Jon) went to the park to play. Their cat Fluffy followed them all the way. As they were going down the slide, they saw a large stray dog chase poor Fluffy up a tree. The dog ran off, but Fluffy would not come down! Finally, Sam climbed the tree and rescued the frightened cat.

1.32 Teacher check:
Words should be written correctly five times each.

1.33 Any order:
a. though
b. throw
c. phone
d. owner

1.34
a. cause (**e** is silent)
b. ready (**a** is silent)
c. phone (**e** is silent)
d. though / (**u**, **g**, and **h** are silent)
e. laugh (**u** is silent)

1.35 join, though, phone

1.36 throw, phone, ready

1.37

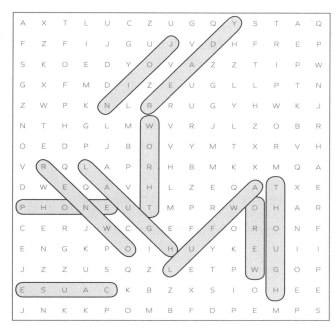

1.38   Teacher check:
Early to bed, early to rise, makes one healthy,
wealthy, and wise.

SELF TEST 1

1.01   no
1.02   yes
1.03   yes
1.04   no
1.05   yes
1.06   Our dog likes to lie on that rug.
1.07   a. asleep
b. broom
c. game
d. idea
e. rug
f. salt
g. tale
h. west
i. yesterday

1.08

Antonyms		Synonyms	
happy	sad	small	tiny
long	short	smile	grin
good	bad	jump	leap
smile	frown	run	jog

1.09

2	joyful	2	notebook
2	today	3	paragraph
1	jump	2	correct
3	holiday	1	night

SECTION 2

2.1	b. not hopeful
2.2	d. hopeful
2.3	e. discouraged
2.4	c. glad
2.5	a. frightened
2.6	Main Street
2.7	blue
2.8	July
2.9	Katie
2.10	changed light bulbs
2.11	cookies and lemonade
2.12	clouds were gathering (Students may include "hot day with no breeze.")
2.13	rumbling of thunder
2.14	Sam is determined to do the job.
2.15	Sam doesn't have enough money for a new bike.
2.16	new in town
2.17	want a new bike
2.18	a friend named Katie
2.19	willing to work
2.20	in the house
2.21	Sam and Katie were friends.
2.22	Sam had just moved to town and wanted a new bike.
2.23	Sam and Katie made signs to hang around town.
2.24	Sam raked the lawn for Mrs. Murphy to earn some money.
2.25	Sam worked hard for Mrs. Murphy.
2.26	He was discouraged but did not give up.
2.27	A storm is coming !
2.28	Where is the flashlight ?
2.29	That huge tree in the backyard fell over !
2.30	Mother turned on the battery powered radio.
2.31	Is the storm over now ?
2.32	b. candies
2.33	c. pennies
2.34	a. ponies
2.35	mysteries
2.36	families
2.37	cities
2.38	discoveries
2.39	parties
2.40	Each set can be in any order:

right	bought	taught	night
bright	thought	caught	fright
sight	brought		might
fight			

2.41	Teacher check: Words should be written correctly five times each.
2.42	sight
2.43	thought
2.44	bought
2.45	brought
2.46	might
2.47	bright
2.48	fright
2.49	right
2.50	Teacher check: Answers will vary. Check for correct sentence structure, capitalization, and punctuation.

SELF TEST 2

2.01	Katie and Sam are friends.
2.02	Sam changed light bulbs in Mrs. Murphy's garage.
2.03	Sam's family moved in July.
2.04	Sam needs jobs to make money for a new bike.
2.05	After Sam got home, it began to storm.
2.06	no
2.07	no
2.08	yes
2.09	no
2.010	yes
2.011	buddies
2.012	bodies
2.013	ponies
2.014	countries
2.015	stories
2.016	pennies
2.017	ladies
2.018	bunnies
2.019	e. Katie
2.020	c. July
2.021	a. Sam
2.022	d. elderly
2.023	b. lemonade and cookies

SECTION 3

3.1	Sam's change of attitude.
3.2	in the late afternoon/early evening
3.3	Katie telling Sam he could make a lot of money.
3.4	Answers will vary but should reflect that the tree is lying on the lawn, uprooted.
3.5	He decided he would help people and not take any payment for his help.
3.6	Sam and his parents stepped outside to take a look at things.
3.7	Katie
3.8	Mrs. Murphy
3.9	Sam
3.10	2, 4, 1, 3

3.11

PERSON	PLACE	THING
Sam	backyard	job
Mother	store	bike
Father	garage	money
Katie	school	tree
Mrs. Murphy	house	signs

3.12	We started our vacation on June 12, 2016.
3.13	I need to use drawing paper, colored pencils, and paints.
3.14	Our snack was popcorn, chocolate cake, and milk.
3.15	Friday will be June 24, 2016.
3.16	I play the piano, organ, trombone, and violin.
3.17	Teacher check: Answers will vary but should include a correctly punctuated series of items.
3.18–3.19	Teacher check: Answer should include the date, with correct punctuation.
3.20	Sam lived with his parents at 1204 E. State Street.
3.21	Sam's friend, Katie, lived one street over at 1202 N. Sycamore Street.
3.22	Katie had a pet goldfish named Howie.
3.23	Mrs. Murphy, who lived at 1210 N. Sycamore Street, needed help.
3.24	She saw Sam and Katie's sign and called Sam's phone number.
3.25	Mrs. Murphy hired Sam to rake her lawn at 1210 N. Sycamore Street.
3.26	Mrs. Murphy had a dog named Nikki and a parrot she called Charlene.
3.27	Mrs. Murphy's grandchildren, Kathleen and Aaron, visited her in April.
3.28	They left on April 28, 2016.
3.29	After that, Mrs. Murphy was lonely, so Sam and Katie cheered her up.

3.30 Teacher check:
Words should be written correctly five times each.

3.31 garage, remember, people, attitude, window, outside, sign, replace, eager, thirty

3.32 a. garages
 b. windows
 c. attitudes
 d. signs

3.33 thirty

3.34 eager, remember

3.35 outside

3.36 people

3.37 replace

3.38

1	2	3
sign	garage	remember
	people	attitude
	window	
	outside	
	replace	
	eager	
	thirty	

3.39 a. mysteries   e. buddies
 b. churches   f. horses
 c. families   g. cities
 d. girls   h. houses

3.40 Teacher check:
Answers will vary, but students should write complete sentences with proper end marks.

SELF TEST 3

3.01 puppies

3.02 windows

3.03 cherries

3.04 storms

3.05 candies

3.06 sisters

3.07 syllables

3.08 churches

3.09 wishes

3.010 boxes

3.011 Danielle goes to Burnside Street School in Bloomington, Indiana.

3.012 Scott lives on Oak Street in a blue house.

3.013 Do you want to go swimming?

3.014 My teacher is Mr. Brady.

3.015 When is Mike's birthday?

3.016 His birthday is July 20, 2005.

3.017 The new family in church came from Washington.

3.018 Grandpa's favorite holiday is Easter.

3.019

8	whale	4	leopard
1	camel	3	kangaroo
5	monkey	2	giraffe
6	parrot	7	snake

3.020 Answers will vary but should include complete sentences and proper end marks.

LIFEPAC TEST

1. 4 "You could really make a lot of cash!"
2. 3 Thunder boomed and lightning zigzagged across the sky.
3. 1 Sam wants a new bike.
4. 2 Mrs. Murphy called Sam to rake and change light bulbs.
5.   5   1
      6   7
      4   3
      2   9
    10   8
6. families
7. goats
8. mysteries
9. garage
10. raking
11. churches
12. bicycles
13. steps
14. ladder
15. shells
16. Teacher check for sentence structure, correct punctuation, and correct capitalization.
17. Mr. Stratton, Katie's father, works for a plumber. He has worked for this plumber since January 3, 2010. He sometimes gets called to work late at night. He works with John, Joe, Ben, and Sally. He takes his lunch along to work. His favorite lunch is a meatball sandwich, potato chips, a banana, and pudding. Mr. Stratton doesn't work on New Year's Day, Easter, Thanksgiving, or Christmas.
18.

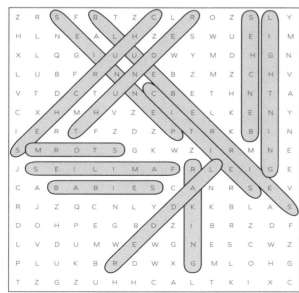

ALTERNATE LIFEPAC TEST

1. armchair
books
chalkboard
dictionary
eraser
games
lights
pencils
students
teacher
2. Josie got a skateboard, a paint set, and a soccer ball for her birthday. She was born on May 4, 2008. She was happy to share her new gifts with Shelley, Mike, Mary, and Erin. They had cake, watermelon, and soda at her party in the park.
3. phone
4. bike
5. please
6. initial
7. cookies
8. laugh
9. riddle
10. storm
11. enough
12. children
13.   r**e**ady
    u**n**tied
    ph**o**ne
    la**u**gh
    thou**g**h
    everyw**h**ere
14. Teacher check:
Check for sentence structure, correct punctuation, and correct capitalization.

SPELLING TEST

1	awful	A skunk has an **awful** smell.	awful
2	cause	The water will **cause** the plant to grow.	cause
3	drew	The artist **drew** a picture for me.	drew
4	ready	He is **ready** to go to town.	ready
5	join	Paul will **join** the team.	join
6	owner	The **owner** of the house is gone.	owner
7	laugh	The clown made us **laugh**.	laugh
8	sight	The plane flew out of our **sight**.	sight
9	right	I know I am **right**.	right
10	fight	Our dog had a **fight** with the cat.	fight
11	bought	My mother **bought** a new coat.	bought
12	thought	He **thought** the answer was right.	thought
13	taught	Father **taught** us to ride a bicycle.	taught
14	caught	Joe **caught** a big fish.	caught
15	night	It is dark at **night**.	night
16	might	If he were older, he **might** understand.	might
17	garage	A new car was parked in the **garage**.	garage
18	people	Many **people** were coming to the picnic.	people
19	replace	A new bulb was purchased to **replace** the broken one in the lamp.	replace
20	sign	We need to find a **sign** for the location of the store.	sign
21	window	Please open the **window** to let some cool air into the room.	window
22	eager	The girl was **eager** to play the game.	eager
23	outside	Two boys stood on the sidewalk **outside** the store.	outside
24	thirty	About **thirty** birds were sitting on the wire.	thirty
25	remember	You must **remember** to bring your lunch to eat.	remember

LANGUAGE ARTS 305

ALTERNATE LIFEPAC TEST

NAME _____

DATE _____

SCORE _____

38
48

Each answer = 1 point

Copy in correct alphabetical order the following things that you find in a classroom.

1.

chalkboard
armchairs
books
pencils
lights

games
erasers
teacher
dictionary
students

_____   _____

_____   _____

_____   _____

_____   _____

_____   _____

Put commas and periods in the correct places in this story.

2.   Josie got a skateboard a paint set and a soccer ball for her birthday She was born on May 4 2008 She was happy to share her new gifts with Shelley Mike Mary and Erin They had cake watermelon and soda at her party in the park

Use these words in the following sentences.

phone	riddle	cookies	laugh	please
storm	children	bike	initial	enough

3. When the _____ rang, I answered it.

4. Sam wanted a new, blue _____ .

5. If you say _____ , your friends are happy to help you.

6. The middle _____ of the name James A. Brown is A.

7. We had _____ and milk for an after school snack.

8. I began to _____ when I heard the joke.

9. A _____ asks a funny question.

10. There were many trees uprooted during the _____ .

11 Sam will continue to save his money until he has _____ to buy the bike.

12. The _____ played in the park.

Put the words in the puzzle.

13. ready   everywhere
      phone   laugh
      though   untied

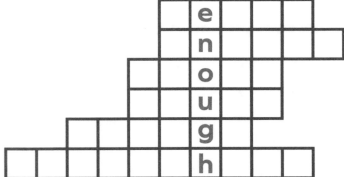

Write a paragraph about one thing.

14. Be sure to use capital letters, periods, commas, and spelling words correctly. Use your best handwriting. Your paragraph will be worth 10 points.

ALTERNATE SPELLING TEST

1	awful	A skunk has an **awful** smell.	awful
2	though	**Though** it was raining, I played outside.	though
3	throw	Please **throw** the ball to the dog.	throw
4	ready	He is **ready** to go to town.	ready
5	phone	Please answer the **phone**.	phone
6	owner	The **owner** of the house is gone.	owner
7	laugh	The clown made us **laugh**.	laugh
8	right	I know I am **right**.	right
9	bright	The light is very **bright**.	bright
10	bought	My mother **bought** a new coat.	bought
11	thought	He **thought** the answer was right.	thought
12	brought	Sue **brought** her lunch to school.	brought
13	taught	Father **taught** us to ride a bicycle.	taught
14	caught	Joe **caught** a big fish.	caught
15	fright	The spider gave the girl a **fright**.	fright
16	garage	A new car was parked in the **garage**.	garage
17	people	Many **people** were coming to the picnic.	people
18	replace	A new bulb was purchased to **replace** the broken one in the lamp.	replace
19	window	Please open the **window** to let some cool air into the room.	window
20	sign	We need to find a **sign** for the location of the store.	sign
21	outside	Two boys stood on the sidewalk **outside** the store.	outside
22	eager	The girl was **eager** to play the game.	eager
23	attitude	The little dog had a friendly **attitude**.	attitude
24	thirty	About **thirty** birds were sitting on the wire.	thirty
25	remember	You must **remember** to bring your lunch to eat.	remember

LANGUAGE ARTS 306

Unit 6: All about Books

TEACHER NOTES

MATERIALS NEEDED FOR LIFEPAC	
Required	Suggested
None	• Bible • dictionary • paper • storybook about a deer • library card and library book • paper or 3" x 5" file cards • drawing paper • pictures • magazines • scissors • crayons • paste • stapler • construction paper or wall paper

ADDITIONAL LEARNING ACTIVITIES

Section 1: The Main Idea

1. Student may read a portion of the parable aloud.

2. Discuss with students the fact that the son was sorry for his sin and turned from it.

3. Learn the songs "Nothing but the Blood" by Robert Lowry and "What a Friend We Have in Jesus" by Joseph Scriven.

4. Make up a puppet show of the parable. Classmates may play the various roles.

5. Draw a picture to illustrate the parable.

Section 2: Parts of a Book

1. Teacher or librarian can show the student how to search the online library catalog.

2. Help the student find a book that he can read and use for his book report.

3. Student may pretend he is a character from a book. A classmate may be another character from the book. Carry on a conversation from the book or make up a dialogue. Remain true to the role assumed.

4. Make your own puppets for the puppet show of an incident in a library book.
   Look in the library for a book on making puppets for ideas and directions.

5. Make a brief outline for the library book. Chapter headings would be the main points. Incidents in the chapters would be the subpoints.

6. Write a real letter to the author of the book. Send it in care of the publisher.

Section 3: Cause and Effect

1. Discuss with students the older brother's attitude.
   Note that in Matthew 6:12–15 Jesus taught forgiveness.

2. Note the students' attitudes on forgiveness.

3. Read the parable in Matthew 7:24–27 and discuss it.

4. Make a mural depicting events in the parable.

5. Learn the song, "The Wise Man and the Foolish Man" by H. D. Loes (*Salvation Songs for Children*).

6. Paint a picture depicting something from one of the parables.

7. Make a poster to advertise the puppet show.

Section 4: Two Meanings

1. Teacher may assist student in making an alternate list of words from which he can derive a haiku poem.

2. Assist student in hearing the long vowel sounds in the spelling words.

3. Class may do choral readings of poems.

4. Several students may do a study on Japanese culture and customs and present a report to the group.

5. Students may practice reading two or three poems from a book of poems. Tape record the readings and listen to them in order to note areas for improvement. Students may then re-record the readings to be played for the class or read the poems to the class.

6. Memorize a poem you have read and enjoyed.

7. Make a collection of poems on a particular subject (colors, feelings, seasons, holidays, time, etc.). Write them in a notebook and draw illustrations for them.

8. Check each student's book of poems for covers, title page, separate page for each poem written in proper form, illustration for each poem, and neatness of handwriting.

Administer the LIFEPAC Spelling Test.

The test is provided in this Teacher's Guide.
Evaluate the tests and review the words the students spelled incorrectly.
If necessary, review all of the words in the unit to prepare for the alternate spelling test.
Administer the Alternate LIFEPAC Spelling test that is provided in this Teacher's Guide.

Administer the LIFEPAC Test.

The test is to be administered in one session. Give no help except with directions.
Evaluate the tests and review areas where the students have done poorly.
Review the pages and activities that stress the concepts tested.
If necessary, administer the Alternate LIFEPAC Test.

ANSWER KEYS

SECTION 1

1.1 The younger son was sorry for his sin, and his father forgave him.
1.2 b, d, f, g
1.3 a. younger son
b. father
1.4 station
1.5 question
1.6 direction
1.7 invention
1.8 vacation
1.9 mention
1.10 Teacher check
1.11 Example:
I had to peer through the hole to see.
1.12 cheer
1.13 steer

SELF TEST 1

1.01 the most important thing in the story.
1.02 he did as he pleased and spent all his money.
1.03 that he had sinned and was sorry about it.
1.04 small bits of fact.
1.05 a ring, a robe, and shoes for his son.
1.06 taking care of pigs.
1.07 parable
1.08 deer
1.09 invention
1.010 cheer
1.011 direction
1.012 question
1.013 vacation

SECTION 2

2.1   Example: I liked <u>Rabbit Hill</u> the best.
2.2   Example. Mother read <u>Uncle Wiggly</u> to me.
2.3   Example: I did not like <u>A Girl in Norway</u>.
2.4   Teacher check
2.5   Teacher check
2.6   a.   Example: Tim, my friend, likes to work.
         b.   Example: Tim, let's go out and play.
2.7   a.   In my lunch box, I have a sandwich, cookies, and an apple.
         b.   For school, I use a pencil, pen, ruler, crayons, and paper.
         c.   When we went to camp, we needed notebooks, pencils, flashlights, and sleeping bags.
2.8   Teacher check
2.9   Answers will vary.
2.10   Answers will vary.
2.11   Teacher check
2.12   H
           S
           H
           H
           S
           S
           S
           S
           H
           S
           S
           H
           H
           H
           S
           H
           S
           H
           S
           S
           H
           H
           S
           S
           H
           H
           S
2.13   ✓ bridge
2.14   ✓ judge
2.15   ✓ edge

SELF TEST 2

2.01   <u>Runaway Boy</u>
2.02–2.05 Any order:
2.02   He put a sandwich and an apple in a bag.
2.03   He put on his coat.
2.04   He walked down the street.
2.05   He began to be sorry for being bad.
         or He turned around and went home.
2.06   title
2.07   author
2.08   illustrator
2.09   topic
2.010   capital letters
2.011   a.   Savage Dog
         b.   A Cat Named Bibs
         c.   Nip and Tuck
2.012   Savage Dog, A Cat Named Bibs, and Nip and Tuck.
2.013   Buddy, my friend, likes to play football.
2.014   Buddy, my friend likes to play football.
2.015–2.019 Any order:
2.015   big
2.016   dog
2.017   go
2.018   get
2.019   good
2.020–2.024 Any order:
2.020   page
2.021   rage
2.022   large
2.023   magic
2.024   edge
2.025   the most important thing in the story.
2.026   small bits of facts.

SECTION 3

3.1   2
          4
          1
          5
          3

3.2   4
          1
          5
          3
          2

3.3   She said, "Ouch."
3.4   They killed the calf.
3.5   The servant said there was a feast.
3.6   Younger son put on new clothes and a ring.
3.7   Someone knocked at the door.
3.8   He was jealous of younger brother.
3.9   Younger son had come home.
3.10   He had spent all his money and time with bad friends.
3.11   Answers will vary.
3.12   Teacher check
3.13   calf
3.14   calves
3.15   half
3.16   halves
3.17   leaf
3.18   leaves
3.19   thief
3.20   thieves
3.21   fairy
3.22   Across   Down
          1. fair   2. repair
          3. pair
          4 air
          5. hair
          6. stair

          Puzzle word: repair

SELF TEST 3

3.01   3
          2
          1
          5
          4

3.02   The room was bright.
3.03   The ball went through the air.
3.04   The pencil did not get sharpened.
3.05   He was hungry.
3.06   Perry dropped the glass.
3.07   The alarm clock did not ring.
3.08   a. calf
          b. calves
3.09   a. half
          b. halves
3.010 a. leaves
          b. leaf
3.011 air
3.012 fair
3.013 a. hair
          b. pair
3.014 a. repair
          b. stair
3.015 directions
3.016 invention
3.017 Janice, my friend, is moving away.
3.018 Janice, my friend is moving away.

SECTION 4

4.1 Example:
Rub a dub dub, Three men in a tub.
4.2 Teacher check
4.3 read
4.4 read
4.5 live
4.6 live
4.7 tear
4.8 tear
4.9 Teacher check
4.10 Teacher check
4.11 piece
pie
received
weighs
4.12 A. eight
eighteen
eighty
sleigh
weigh
E. believe
chief
field
thief
piece
E. ceiling
either
neither
receive
seize
I. die
fries
lie
pie
tie
4.13 ei
ceiling
either
neither
receive
seize
ie
believe
chief
field
thief
piece

4.14 a. believe — to accept as true or real
chief — the person highest in rank
field — a piece of land with few or no trees
piece — a part of something
thief — one who steals

b. ceiling — the top of a room
either — one or the other of two
neither — not the one nor the other
receive — to take
seize — to take hold of suddenly

c. die — to stop living
fries — a dish of fried potatoes
lie — an untrue statement
pie — a baked food
tie — to fasten with cord

d. eight — 8
eighteen — 18
eighty — 80
sleigh — a wagon with runners
weigh — to find the weight of

4.15 Teacher check
4.16 eight
4.17 believe
4.18 either
4.19 neither, lie

SELF TEST 4

4.01   parable
          he pleased
          spent
4.02   left
4.03   bad
4.04   bad
4.05   sinned
4.06   angry
4.07   older son
4.08   book
4.09   haiku
4.010 poem
4.011 (steer)
4.012 (hair)
4.013 (pair)
4.014 (fair)
4.015 a. (calf)
          b. (calves)
4.016 a. (leaf)
          b. (leaves)
4.017 (Two Wrongs)
4.018 right   thought   polite
          fight   ought
4.019 5
4.020 5
          7
          5

4.021 a. eight
              eighteen
              eighty
              weigh
              sleigh
          b. believe
              chief
              field
              piece
              thief
          c. ceiling
              either
              neither
              receive
              seize
          d. tie
              lie
              fries
              pie
              die
4.022 title
4.023 author
4.024 illustrator
4.025 topic
4.026 capital letters

LIFEPAC TEST

1. parable
2. The young man sinned by doing as he pleased and spending all his money.
3. yes
   no
   yes
4. He could not see.
5. He fell from the boat when it tipped.
6. 2
   1
   5
   4
   3
7. question
8. mention
9. deer
10. a. half
    b. half
11. thief
12. H S
    H S
    S H
    H S
    S H
    H S
13. a. eight
    b. ceiling
    c. piece
    d. sleigh
14. title
15. poem
16. topic
17. author
18. illustrator
19. Mother Goose
20. Holy Bible
21. Sandy and the Seashells
22. Tim, my pal came with me.
23. Tim, my pal, came with me.
24. crayons, pencil, paper, scissors, ruler, and paste.
25. two, shoe, four, door

ALTERNATE LIFEPAC TEST

1. parable
2. The younger son did as he pleased and spent all his money foolishly.
3. yes
4. no
5. yes
6. no
7. yes
8. yes
9. The man shivered and buttoned his coat.
10. No one ate the hot dogs.
11. b
12. a
13. e
14. c
15. d
16. question
17. vacation
18. deer
19. piece
20. illustrator
21. topic
22. author
23. title
24. poem
25. Child's Garden of Verses
26. The Three Bears
27. Mr.Top Dog
28. H
29. H
30. S
31. H
32. S
33. H
34. S
35. S
36. H
37. S
38. H
39. S
40. Example:
    plants, shovel, rake, water, pail, and hoe
41. Mac, my friend, plays soccer.
42. Mac, my friend plays soccer.
43. day, way, best, blessed
44. calf, calves
45. thief

SPELLING TEST

1	deer	We saw a **deer** in the forest.	deer
2	veer	The driver had to **veer** into the open lane to avoid an accident.	veer
3	direction	We gave the man the **direction** to our house.	direction
4	mention	He could not find a word to rhyme with **mention**.	mention
5	station	The bus was at the **station** this morning.	station
6	age	What do you think is the **age** of that house?	age
7	page	The story is on **page** twenty.	page
8	bridge	We had to cross the **bridge** to get over the river.	bridge
9	judge	God is the **judge** of the universe.	judge
10	girl	The **girl** with long hair sat across from me.	girl
11	calf	The newborn **calf** began to walk.	calf
12	leaf	The **leaf** fell from the tree.	leaf
13	calves	How many **calves** were born?	calves
14	leaves	The **leaves** are beginning to fall.	leaves
15	air	We need **air** to breathe.	air
16	fairy	This story is about some elves and a **fairy**.	fairy
17	pair	He bought a new **pair** of shoes.	pair
18	stair	He climbed the final **stair** to the top.	stair
19	chief	His grandfather was a **chief** of a great Native American nation.	chief
20	thief	The **thief** was sentenced to prison.	thief
21	ceiling	The **ceiling** was not very high.	ceiling
22	neither	**Neither** one of the boys wanted to go.	neither
23	seize	The police will **seize** the thief.	seize
24	fries	She **fries** her chicken.	fries
25	eighteen	My sister will be **eighteen** tomorrow.	eighteen

LANGUAGE ARTS 306

ALTERNATE LIFEPAC TEST

NAME _____

DATE _____

SCORE _____

38
47

Each answer = 1 point

Circle the word that makes the sentence correct. Write it on the line.

1. In Luke chapter 15, we read the _____ that Jesus Christ
told to explain a truth. (tale / parable)

Check the setence that tells what the story was about.

2. _____ The younger son did as he pleased and spent all his
money foolishly.

_____ There was a famine in the land.

_____ The farmer hired the younger son to tend the pigs.

Write *yes* or *no* before each sentence.

3. _____ The younger son said, "Give me my share of the property."

4. _____ He traveled by camel on his trip.

5. _____ He had bad friends who helped spend his money.

6. _____ He helped feed some starving people.

7. _____ He began to think about and feel sorry for his sins.

8. _____ He wanted to ask his father for a job as a servant.

Draw a line from the cause to the effect.

Cause	Effect
9. A cold wind blew.	The man took off his coat.
	The man shivered and buttoned his coat.
	The man fanned himself with his hand.

Cause	Effect
10. The hotdogs burned up.	He put catsup on the hotdogs.
	He put the hotdogs on a plate.
	No one ate the hotdogs.

Do you remember what happened in the parable in Luke chapter 15? Put the following sentences in order. Draw a line from the number 1 to the letter of the sentence that tells what happened first and so on.

11.	1	a.	Younger son spent his money on fun and bad friends.
12.	2	b.	Younger son took his money and left home.
13.	3	c.	Father forgave his son and was glad he was home.
14.	4	d.	Older son was angry and upset over his brother's return.
15.	5	e.	Younger son thought of his sin and was sorry.

Draw a circle around the word that best completes the sentence. Write it on the line.

16. He asked a _____ about a car.
(invention / question)

17. We usually go on _____ when school is closed.
(mention / vacation)

18. The _____ was walking slowly across the clearing.
(deer / dear)

19. I'd like to have a _____ of pie.
(peace / piece)

Read the words below. Write the word that matches the meaning on the line.

> author   poem   illustrator   title   topic

20. Artist who makes pictures to be used in books. _____

21. Subject that people think, write, or talk about. _____

22. Person who writes books, poems, or stories. _____

23. The name of a book, poem, picture, or song. _____

24. A story that rhymes. _____

Write the following book titles on the lines using capital letters where needed.

25. child's garden of verses _____

26. the three bears _____

27. mr. top dog _____

Write *H* after each word that has the hard *g* sound as in *goat*.
Write *S* after each word that has the hard *g* sound as in *giant*.

28. dog _____   **34.** judge _____

29. get _____   **35.** strange _____

30. giraffe _____   **36.** gave _____

31. begin _____   **37.** gingerbread _____

32. large _____   **38.** goodbye _____

33. gone _____   **39.** danger _____

Write the following words in a sentence using commas.

> plants   shovel   rake   water   pail   hoe

40. To get my garden ready, I need _____

_____

Put commas in the sentences to show that

41. Mac is my friend.   Mac my friend plays soccer.

42. Mac is being spoken to.   Mac my friend plays soccer.

Underline the rhyming words in the following poem.

43. This is a new day.

Try in every way.

To do your very best

And you will be blessed.
.

Draw a circle around the word that makes the sentence correct. Write it on the line.

44. We sold one brown _____ and the two white _____ .
          (calf / calves)   (calf / calves)

45. The squirrel was the _____ who took the walnuts.
          (thief / thieves)

ALTERNATE SPELLING TEST

1	cheer	He gave a **cheer** for his team.	cheer
2	steer	Let me **steer** the car.	steer
3	invention	Bob went to look at the scientist's new **invention**.	invention
4	question	The teacher asked Bob a **question**.	question
5	vacation	We are going on **vacation** next week.	vacation
6	edge	He sat on the **edge** of his chair.	edge
7	game	Dad wanted to watch the football **game**.	game
8	goat	The **goat** tried to jump over the fence.	goat
9	half	I gave Sue **half** of my cake.	half
10	thief	A **thief** stole our money.	thief
11	halves	I will divide the cake into **halves**.	halves
12	thieves	There are a lot of **thieves** in this city.	thieves
13	fair	Our family plans to go to the city **fair**.	fair
14	repair	Fred will have to **repair** the broken toy.	repair
15	believe	We **believe** that Jesus is God.	believe
16	field	This **field** is long.	field
17	piece	She gave him a **piece** of her candy.	piece
18	either	You can **either** go to the park or the zoo.	either
19	receive	How many presents will you **receive**?	receive
20	lie	Do not tell anyone a **lie**.	lie
21	tie	She knows how to **tie** a fancy knot.	tie
22	eight	I have **eight** brothers.	eight
23	eighty	My grandfather is **eighty** years old.	eighty
24	sleigh	Tonight we are going to ride a **sleigh**.	sleigh
25	weigh	How much do you **weigh**?	weigh

LANGUAGE ARTS 307

Unit 7: Reading and Writing

TEACHER NOTES

MATERIALS NEEDED FOR LIFEPAC	
Required	Suggested
None	• tagboard • newsprint • crayons • maps of states

ADDITIONAL LEARNING ACTIVITIES

Section 1: Main Ideas

1. Read the Parable of the Good Samaritan (Luke 10:30-37). Put the main idea into words and add details using complete sentences. Write in best handwriting.

2. Continue instructions with other examples of singular and plural nouns.

3. List nouns; see if they can be combined to make compound words. Exchange lists with other students.

4. Make puzzles, such as Seek and Find, with names of fish, tools, vegetables, and so on.

5. Copy the following Bible verses in your best handwriting for display on the bulletin board.

    Psalm 139:23-24

    Psalm 119:33

    Psalm 51:1-2

    Psalm 91:1-2

Section 2: Sequence

1. In pairs, make crossword puzzles to share with others.

2. Make a map of a state and show the interesting places to see in it. Color the map.

3. Make a map of buried treasure. Be sure to make the clues for where it is buried definite.

4. Write out directions to

    a. make a clock,

    b. clean the refrigerator,

    c. ride a bicycle, or

    d. find a lost coin (see Luke 15:8-10 for hints).

Section 3: Pronouns and Suffixes

1. Make a chart for person and number of pronouns.

2. Make a chart of properly formed letters, both lowercase and uppercase, to put on your bulletin board at home.

3. Using the situations and characters from the stories in the LIFEPAC, (page 4, pages 21 and 22, page 41) continue the ideas found there. Urge the use of plural nouns and good handwriting.

Section 4: Reading a Map

1. Make a map of the place where you went (or would like to go) on your vacation.

Administer the LIFEPAC Spelling Test.

The test is provided in this Teacher's Guide.
Evaluate the tests and review the words the students spelled incorrectly.
If necessary, review all of the words in the unit to prepare for the alternate spelling test.
Administer the Alternate LIFEPAC Spelling test that is provided in this Teacher's Guide.

Administer the LIFEPAC Test.

The test is to be administered in one session. Give no help except with directions.
Evaluate the tests and review areas where the students have done poorly.
Review the pages and activities that stress the concepts tested.
If necessary, administer the Alternate LIFEPAC Test.

ANSWER KEYS

SECTION 1

1.1 Example:
God provides for all His creatures' needs.

1.2
a. church
b. teacher
c. noon
d. Bethlehem
e. mother
f. camera
g. desk
h. string
i. Tuesday
j. baby
k. school
l. girl
m. squirrel
n. zoo
o. yesterday
p. Tomorrow

1.3
a. boy
b. Mother
c. chicken
d. man
e. school
f. plane
g. year
h. Bob
i. shoe
j. monkey
k. car
l. toy
m. home

1.4 friend's name

1.5
a. trucks
b. horse
c. airplanes
d. giraffes
e. plants
f. apple
g. cupcake
h. flowers
i. benches

1.6 Examples:

Singular noun	Plural noun
walk	birds
dinner	berries
jacket	
leash	
street	
bush	

1.7 Drawings will vary.

1.8
alligators
aprons
bananas
belts
benches
bicycles
brooms
bushes
castles
combs
dimes
edges
flashes
baths
beaches
brushes
frogs
hearts
hitches
inches
jets
foxes
lessons
crosses
machines
churches

1.9

S	P
S	S
S	S
S	S
P	P
S	P
P	S
P	P
S	P
S	S
P	P
P	S

1.10

outdoor	baseball
afternoon	skyscraper
doorway	snowstorm
daydream	workmen
everybody	backyard
football	

1.11   Examples:
We played *football*.
This *afternoon* the sun came out.
Everybody went home.
The *butterfly* was yellow.
The *doorbell* rang.
The *cowboy* rides a horse.
We had a *snowstorm*.
I would like a *cupcake*.

1.12   a. football
           b. butterfly
           c. bedroom
           d. doorbell
           e. cowboy
           f. cupcake

1.13   everybody

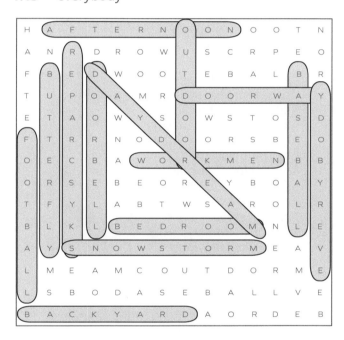

1.14   Teacher check
1.15   Teacher check

SELF TEST 1

1.01   God provides for all His creatures.
1.02   people, places, things, and times
1.03   dog   store
1.04   boy   tricks
1.05   box   shelf
1.06   watch   table
1.07   Mary   Jack
1.08   Examples:
My horse is named Lady.
Let's ride in a spaceship.
We went to California.
1.09   one
1.010 more than one
1.011 elephant
1.012 flower
1.013 yards
1.014 Example:
The big ball flew from his hand.
1.015 Example:
Many kittens ran into the yard.
1.016 lunches
1.017 motorcycles
1.018 foxes
1.019 doors
1.020 crosses
1.021 girls
1.022 dishes
1.023 bikes
1.024 pencils
1.025 tables

SECTION 2

2.1 1. Clean off the back porch.
2. Put toys in the box.
3. Sweep the floor.
4. Straighten up his room.
5. Take trash out and put it in the can.

2.2 Teacher check

2.3 Teacher check

2.4 armies
balconies
batteries
bodies
butterflies
candies
chimneys
groceries
ladies
french fries
donkeys
mysteries
poppies
replies
skies
valleys

2.5 halves
knives
shelves
wives
calves
leaves
thieves
wolves
elves
loaves

2.6 feet
mice
policemen
sheep
snowmen
teeth
fishermen
geese
women
workmen

2.7 Down
1. wives
2. sheep
4. mysteries
7. worries
8. bodies
9. armies
10. candies
12. skies

Across
3. fishermen
5. shelves
6. replies
8. balconies
11. snowmen
12. shells
13. french fries

2.8 Examples:
a. Our dog had four puppies.
b. We will build two snowmen.
c. The monkeys were climbing.
d. How many sheep are in the field?

2.9 a. a car battery
b. six butterflies
c. three knives
d. my wife
f. two thieves
g. a tiny elf
h. fourteen sheep
i. four baby calves
k. the hungry wolf
l. the hungry wolves
m. a mystery
n. a lot of puppies
p. our little kitty
r. the two mice
s. two feet
t. five donkeys
u. one snowman
v. six donkeys
w. many teeth
x. a deep valley
aa. a lot of geese
bb. some workmen
dd. three shelves
ee. french fries
gg. only one table
kk. our country
ll. six flies
mm. two halves
nn. some chimneys

2.10 Examples:
takes care of
a living person or animal
something to hold an animal
a little juicy fruit with seeds
rubbish
a short time
entrance to building

2.11 a. dragged or grabbed
       b. clapping
       c. wrapping
       d. hugged
       e. tagged
       f. nodding
2.12 a. shining
       b. decided
       c. invited
       d. measured
       e. sharing
       f. noticed
2.13 Teacher check
2.14 Teacher check
2.15 Teacher check

SELF TEST 2

2.01 friend   (bicycles)
       road   (tracks)
       town   (trains)
       mom
       railroad
       train
       park
       town
2.02–2.05 Teacher check
2.06 armies
2.07 worries
2.08 donkeys
2.09 valleys
2.010 bodies
2.011 chimneys
2.012 halves
2.013 elves
2.014 loaves
2.015 men
2.016 geese
2.017 batteries
2.018 tagged
2.019 Example: Sue tagged Joan.
2.020 hugged
2.021 Example: Mom hugged Sue.
2.022 shining
2.023 Example: The sun is shining today.
2.024 wrapping
2.025 Example: She is wrapping presents.
2.026 raising
2.027 noticed
2.028 served

SECTION 3

3.1 Example:
A monster lives in the lot. He's big and ugly. He likes animals, but not people. He chases people away.

3.2 Example:
Big sister told funny stories but the children ran on home. The child telling the story remembered God will always be with you.

3.3 Example:
We don't go to school on Saturday or Sunday. We have other things to do on those days.

3.4 Teacher check

3.5
a. She got milk and bread.
b. She and I saw the animals.
c. He went to the park.
d. They did a good job.
e. We got tired.
f. Give the bat to them.
g. Tell them about school.
h. It has many offices.
i. He trained his dog.

3.6 Any order:
a. we
b. I
c. it
d. you
e. she
f. us *or* my, me, he, them

3.7 watch
3.8 Mom
3.9 Dad
3.10 Kathy and Ken
3.11 teacher and I
3.12 boys and girls
3.13 cake
3.14 shoes
3.15 Janie
3.16 Tom
3.17 bigger
3.18 taller
3.19 smartest
3.20 highest
3.21 fastest
3.22 faster
3.23 older
3.24 biggest
3.25 shortest
3.26 Example:
This kitten is the cutest animal here.

3.27 Example:
I feel weaker after the game.

3.28 Example:
I don't know the richest person in the world.

3.29 Example:
These woods are thicker than at home.

3.30 Example:
I'd like a riper apple, please.

3.31 Drawings will vary.
3.32 Drawings will vary.
3.33 Drawings will vary.
3.34 Drawings will vary.

3.35
a. bigger
b. longest
c. thinner
d. swiftest
e. dimmest
f. neater
g. taller
h. weaker

3.36
a. weaker
b. richer
c. thicker
d. riper
e. cooler
f. fresher
g. weakest
h. richest
i. thickest
j. ripest
k. coolest
l. thinnest

3.37
a. Example:
This plum is riper than the last one I ate.
b. Example:
Today is cooler than yesterday.
c. Example:
The air seems fresher today.
d. Example:
This rope is the weakest rope on the boat.
e. Example:
I think swimming is the coolest sport.
f. Example:
This paper is the thinnest paper I have had.

3.38 Teacher check
3.39 Teacher check

SELF TEST 3

3.01 everybody
understand
bedroom
3.02 walked
3.03 shopped
3.04 grinned
3.05 slipped
3.06 slapping
3.07 sneezing
3.08 wiping
3.09 noticing
3.010 wives
3.011 teeth
3.012 policemen
3.013 sheep
3.014 fact
3.015 fiction
3.016 fact
3.017 fiction
3.018 fact
3.019 fiction
3.020 (They)
(It)
(its)
(We)
(our)
(She)
(it)
(they)
(her)
(I)
(you)
(she)
(it)
(their)
(it)
(I)
(we)
(it)
(their)
(me)
(We)
(it)
(it)
(we)
(it)
(it)

3.021 cuter
3.022 fresher
3.023 dimmest
3.024 calmer
3.025 shorter
3.026 neatest
3.027 bigger
3.028 longer
3.029 weaker

SECTION 4

4.1   Teacher check

4.2
- a. twenty
- b. southwest
- c. east
- d. northwest
- e. north
- f. west
- g. south
- h. south
- i. west
- j. Answers will vary.

4.3   Answers will vary.

4.4   Examples:
- a. Go north on C Street. Turn right on Second Street. Cross B Street and A Street.
- b. Go east on Fourth Street to B Street. Go north on B Street to Main Street. Turn northeast on Main.
  Or, go east on Fourth Street to A Street. Go north on A Street to First Street.
- c. Go east on Fourth Street to A Street. Go north on A Street to Third Street.
- d. Go north on C Street to the corner of C Street and First Street.
- e. Go north on C Street to Third Street. Go east on Third Street to B Street. Go north on B Street to Bill's.
- f. Go north on C Street to Second Street. Go west on Second Street.

4.5
- a. north
- b. east
- c. south
- d. west
- e. south
- f. north
- g. east

4.6   Teacher check

4.7

42 E. Brown Road
Mesa, Arizona
May 10, 2016

Box 758
Belén, New Mexico
February 3, 2016

7576 Boon Street
Tulsa, Oklahoma
June 25, 2016

115 Crane Street
Johnstown, Pennsylvania
June 5, 2016

4.8
- a. Dear Mary,
- b. Dear Lester,
- c. Dear Mr. Bowman,
- d. Dear Aunt Jean,
- e. Dear Mrs. Rodriguez,
- f. Dear Mr. and Mrs. Owens,

4.9
- a. no
- b. yes
- c. yes
- d. no

4.10
- a. Yours truly,
- b. Love,
- c. Your daughter,
- d. Sincerely,
- e. With love,
- f. Your son,

4.11–4.13 Signatures will vary.

4.14   Teacher check

4.15   Teacher check

4.16   courage or scatter

4.17   address
scatter
taxicab

4.18   golden
notice
radio

4.19   straw
fault

4.20   Teacher check

4.21   Teacher check

SELF TEST 4

4.01   Answers will vary.

4.02   Example:
246 South Sirrine
Mesa, Arizona
January 7, 2016

4.03   Example: Your friend,

4.04   Example: Dear Daddy,

4.05   Answers will vary.

4.06   east

4.07   north or northwest

4.08   west or southwest

4.09   northwest
northeast
southeast
southwest

4.010 walk north or northeast

4.011
a. heading
b. greeting
c. body
d. closing
e. signature

4.012 d

4.013 b

4.014 g

4.015 f

4.016 k

4.017 c

4.018 e

4.019 i

4.020 h

4.021 a

4.022 m

LIFEPAC TEST

1. noun
2. main
3. singular
4. plural
5. a. s
   b. es
6. letter
7. trash
8. pronoun
9. friendly
10. compound
11. Example:
    Walk south on Green Avenue.
    Turn east on Bird Street. Go to corner
    of Bird Street and Orange Avenue.
12. Example:
    Walk south on Green Avenue.
    Turn east on Kangaroo Street.
13. get something to eat or go to school
14. get a book to read
15. Examples:
    a. teacher
    b. firemen
16. a. park
    b. zoos
17. a. elephant
    b. tables
18. She does not go to school.
19. She put pink icing on it.
20. walked
21. oldest
22. taller
23. smaller
24. sobbing
25. houses
26. monkeys
27. baby
28. plants

ALTERNATE LIFEPAC TEST

1. yes
2. yes
3. no
4. yes
5. yes
6. yes
7. yes
8. yes
9. no
10. yes
11. yes
12. yes
13.–15. Examples:
13. <u>People</u>
    woman
    weatherperson
14. <u>Places</u>
    yard
    school
15. <u>Things</u>
    picture
    street
16. houses
17. monkeys
18. baby
19. plants
20.–23. Teacher check
24. He/She/It jumped, and I fell.
25. He came home with a new car.
26. wasting
27. shorter
28. writing
29. tallest
30. begged

SPELLING TEST

1	outdoor	Volleyball can be an **outdoor** game.	outdoor
2	doorway	Susan was standing in the **doorway**.	doorway
3	baseball	The **baseball** team won their game.	baseball
4	everybody	**Everybody** had fun at the party.	everybody
5	workmen	John watched the **workmen** repair the road.	workmen
6	butterfly	The **butterfly** landed on the flower.	butterfly
7	snowstorm	After the **snowstorm**, we played outside.	snowstorm
8	doorbell	My sister rang the **doorbell**.	doorbell
9	dragged	The dog **dragged** the bone across the yard.	dragged
10	hugged	Grandma **hugged** me.	hugged
11	clapping	The audience is **clapping** very loudly.	clapping
12	decided	I **decided** to wear my blue shirt.	decided
13	invited	John was **invited** to the party.	invited
14	noticed	Jim **noticed** that the tree had fallen down.	noticed
15	sharing	The boys were **sharing** their toys.	sharing
16	shining	The stars are **shining** brightly.	shining
17	weaker	Bob is **weaker** than Joe.	weaker
18	thicker	That lawn is **thicker** than this one.	thicker
19	cooler	It is **cooler** in the shade of the tree.	cooler
20	weakest	That one is the **weakest** of the two strings.	weakest
21	thickest	I have the **thickest** notebook in the class.	thickest
22	coolest	Yesterday was the **coolest** day of the year.	coolest
23	appear	Falling stars **appear** in the sky.	appear
24	beneath	We found the ball **beneath** a bush.	beneath
25	breath	The doctor told me to take a deep **breath**.	breath
26	courage	He has the **courage** to do the task.	courage
27	fault	No one was at **fault** for the accident.	fault
28	notice	I **notice** you have a new sweater.	notice
29	scatter	The wind will **scatter** the seeds.	scatter
30	straw	I drank my soda with a **straw**.	straw

LANGUAGE ARTS 307

ALTERNATE LIFEPAC TEST

NAME _____

DATE _____

SCORE _____

26
33

Each answer = 1 point

Write *yes* **or** *no.*

1. _____ A noun names a person, place, or thing.

2. _____ A singular noun is one person, place, or thing.

3. _____ A plural noun names one person, place, or thing.

4. _____ A compound word is a longer word made up of two short words.

5. _____ The word *awhile* means for a short time.

6. _____ A *creature* can be a person.

7. _____ A *symbol* can be a picture or a word that stands for something else.

8. _____ A *pronoun* is a word that takes the place of a noun.

9. _____ A singular pronoun takes the place of a lot of people.

10. _____ Plural pronouns can be words like *they, us, them, we, their,* and *our.*

11. _____ A friendly letter had five parts: heading, greeting, body, closing, and signature.

12. _____ To make singular nouns into plural nouns we sometimes add the suffixes -*s* and -*es.*

Write two nouns under each heading.

13. People   **14.** Places   **15.** Things

_____   _____   _____

_____   _____   _____

Choose the correct singular or plural nouns from the box to fit the sentences.

houses	baby	donkeys	elephant	monkeys	plants

16. The _____ on our street are painted white.

17. We saw eight _____ on bars at the zoo.

18. Our neighbor has a new _____ .

19. How many _____ are growing in your yard?

Look at this map. Then follow the instructions. Use the symbols to answer the questions.

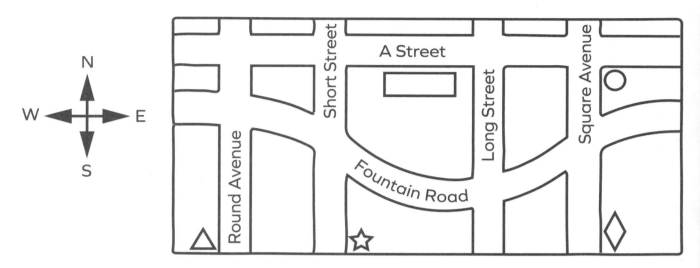

20. Start at △ . Go north to A street. Turn east. Cross Short Street but don't cross long street. You will find a _____ there.

21. Start at ☆ . Go north to Fountain Road. Go east to Square Avenue. Go south on Square Avenue. You find a _____ .

22. Start at △ . Go north to A Street. Turn east to Square Avenue. Go south to the end of Square Avenue. At the corner, you will find a

_____ .

23. Start at △ . Go north to Fountain Road. Go east to Short Street. Turn south on Short Street. You will find a _____ .

Rewrite the second sentence on each line. Use a pronoun in place of the noun to make it sound better.

24. The horse was afraid. *The horse* jumped, and I fell.

_____

25. Father went to town. *Father* came home with a new car.

_____

Add the suffixes *-ed, -ing, -er,* **and** *-est* **to words in the box.**
Write words to fit in the sentences.

write	short	talk	beg	waste	tall

26. The baby is _____ sugar by pouring it on the table.

27. That basketball player is _____ that I am.

28. I am _____ a letter to my sister at camp.

29. My friend is the _____ boy in our class.

30. My dog _____ for his food tonight.

ALTERNATE SPELLING TEST

1	afternoon	In the **afternoon**, I will study for my test.	afternoon
2	daydream	My teacher told me not to **daydream**.	daydream
3	cupcake	There was a **cupcake** in my lunch.	cupcake
4	football	We went to the **football** game.	football
5	backyard	My dog plays in our **backyard**.	backyard
6	skyscraper	We rode the elevator to the top of the **skyscraper**.	skyscraper
7	bedroom	Our **bedroom** is upstairs.	bedroom
8	cowboy	The **cowboy** rode his horse.	cowboy
9	grabbed	She **grabbed** the package before it dropped.	grabbed
10	tagged	John **tagged** the tree.	tagged
11	dipping	Mother was **dipping** the clothes in the washer.	dipping
12	nodding	Dad was **nodding** his approval.	nodding
13	wrapping	The girls are **wrapping** his gift.	wrapping
14	decided	I **decided** to wear my blue shirt.	decided
15	measured	The clerk **measured** the fabric.	measured
16	proving	The Bible helped me in **proving** my point.	proving
17	sneezing	Judy started **sneezing** when she smelled the flower.	sneezing
18	richer	This is the **richer** of the two colors.	richer
19	riper	This is the **riper** of the two apples.	riper
20	fresher	This orange is **fresher** than the pear.	fresher
21	richest	Mr. George is the **richest** man in our town.	richest
22	ripest	The **ripest** apple is hanging on the tree.	ripest
23	thinnest	Sam is the **thinnest** boy in our class.	thinnest
24	address	My **address** is written on the envelope.	address
25	beneath	We found the ball **beneath** a bush.	beneath
26	draw	Sally will **draw** a picture of the horse.	draw
27	church	On Sunday, we will go to **church**.	church
28	golden	The color of the ring was **golden**.	golden
29	radio	John received a **radio** for his birthday	radio
30	straw	I drank my soda with a **straw**.	straw

LANGUAGE ARTS 308

Unit 8: Reading Skills

TEACHER NOTES

MATERIALS NEEDED FOR LIFEPAC	
Required	Suggested
None	• drawing paper • tagboard • lightweight cardboard • picture of parade • comic strips from newspaper • large cardboard box • banner paper • dowel rods • bread • peanut butter • book of plays • paper bags or popsicle sticks • small animals or pictures of animals • flowers • manila envelopes

ADDITIONAL LEARNING ACTIVITIES

Section 1: Sequence and Order

1. Discuss these questions with your class.

    a. What do we celebrate on July Fourth?

    b. What kinds of activities are there on the Fourth of July?

    c. Can you describe a Fourth of July parade?

    d. Have you been to a barbecue? What is it?

    e. What happens at a rodeo?

    f. How do we put a story "in order" (sequence)?

    g. What are adjectives?

    h. Can you name some words that are adjectives?

2. Cut comic strips into individual "frames." Paste each frame on a piece of tagboard for easy handling. Ask students to put them in sequence.

3. Show a picture of one feature of a parade. Ask students to write the sequence of events either before or after the picture.

4. Cut paper dolls from construction paper; then cut each doll in half lengthwise. On left side of doll print an adjective; on right side print a noun (see the following suggestions).
   Ask students to match an adjective with a noun. See how many different combinations they can find.

Adjectives		**Nouns**	
pretty	short	bird	fence
red	big	girls	hippo
ugly	many	boys	man
tall	two	horses	rose
fat	few	hill	monster

5. Cut a large cardboard box to resemble a television set. Have students make a show on strips of paper by pasting at least six scenes together. Two students may show the roll to the whole class (by rolling the ends up on dowel sticks).

6. Have students draw and color a large picture of a rodeo or a parade. They will write the sequence of the events.

7. Have students use salt dough to make a model of some character in the rodeo or parade.

8. Tell students to pretend they are in a rodeo, they are cowboys, or members of a parade band. Ask them to write a story about a rodeo or parade as if they were in it. They should include adjectives of sight, sound, and smell and verbs of action.

Section 2: Detail and Compare

1. Discuss these questions with your class.

    a. What is the main idea of a story?

    b. What do we mean by details in writing or reading?

    c. What suffixes do we use with adjectives for comparison?

    d. Which suffix do we use when comparing two things?

    e. What are compound words?

    f. Can you name some compound words?

2. Here is a three-part activity:

    a. Ask students to give you adjectives to describe their schoolroom. Write these on the chalkboard or a chart.

    b. Have students write sentences with these words to compare their room with the office or cafeteria.

    c. Then have them write sentences comparing their room to other classrooms in the school.

3. Ask students to be newspaper writers. Have them choose events from their classroom experience. Be sure they use a single paragraph for each main idea and fill out the story with details. These articles can be duplicated and distributed as the class newspaper.

4. Have groups gather leaves and bring them to school. Each group mounts the leaves on tagboard and then exchanges them with another group. Allow time for each group to take turns describing their own or another group's leaves, using accurate adjectives.

5. Have students plant bird seed in milk containers (½-gallon size). As the plants grow, have groups keep a diary to compare the growth of the plants, both with other plants and with the same plant a week later. Use good adjectives.

6. Have students make pictures of members of their families. Let other students use these pictures to fit adjectives to the pictures. They may also write sentences to describe the family members.

7. Ask students to choose a character from the Bible (Jesus, Amos, Job, Mary, etc.) and write a paragraph to describe that person.

8. Ask students to write directions for making a peanut butter sandwich.
   Follow directions EXACTLY, illustrating with jar of peanut butter and loaf of bread.
   (Ask, "Do we have a sandwich?" if the result is the jar on top of the bread.)
   Rewrite the instructions if necessary. Then, follow the instructions, and eat the result.

Section 3: Reading Drama

1. Discuss these questions with your class.

   a. What is a drama?

   b. How is drama different from other stories?

   c. What is the plot of a play?

   d. What is the setting of a play?

   e. How do we find out about things happening someplace where we can't see?

   f. What are characters in a play?

   g. What are verbs?

   h. Can you name some verbs?

2. Find a short play in a child's book or magazine. Help the class give the play for another class.

3. Draw a baseball diamond on a large piece of tagboard. Make cards with root words. Put the game board on the floor and stack the cards at each base and at home. Split the class into two teams. List prefixes and suffixes on the board under the name of each team. To play the game, one team member takes the first card from home plate and tries to find a suffix or prefix from his team's list. If he cannot, he is out and the next player comes "to bat." If the first student can make a word, he goes to first base and tries again with the stack there. The same procedure is used until he gets back to home plate for a run. He can be put out at any base. After three outs, let the other team bat.

4. Have each group choose a Bible story and tell it to another class by using paper bag or stick puppets.

5. From drawings by students showing action verbs, let others label the pictures appropriately. They may exchange papers and use different verbs.

6. From Bible stories they read, let the students dramatize events or parables by writing a script showing both action and dialogue. Ask them to draw a stage setting for their drama.

7. Bring a small animal (bird, gerbil, bunny, turtle, etc.) or pictures of animals to school. Ask students to draw a picture of the animal and then use verbs about these animals in sentences to accompany the drawing.

8. Students may write a short play to be presented to the other students by stick or paper bag puppets. The written copy should use proper dialogue form, with proper spelling, punctuation, and capitalization.

9. Students may write a familiar Bible story in their own words.

10. Students may write a paragraph to describe their favorite animals. Encourage the use of adjectives.

Administer the LIFEPAC Spelling Test.

Administer the LIFEPAC Test.

ANSWER KEYS

SECTION 1

1.1   five, seven, nine
one, two, three, four, five, six, seven, eight, nine, ten

1.2   a. 3
b. 5
c. 1
d. 6
e. 4
f. 2

1.3   a. the funny clown
b. the rodeo queen and her princesses
c. the band
d. the old cars

1.4   a. 1
b. 5
c. 3
d. 6
e. 2
f. 4

1.5   4, 1, 2, 3
or 4, 1, 3, 2

1.6   Teacher check

1.7   Last summer, we went to visit Grandma and Grandpa on the farm. I helped Grandma gather eggs. My brother helped haul the hay. All too soon, it was time to leave. On the way home, we saw a deer beside the road.

1.8–1.19 Examples:

1.8   two, coats

1.9   many, pigs

1.10 All, friends

1.11 few, mittens

1.12 six, shirts

1.13 Most, people

1.14 several, dresses

1.15 Eight, children

1.16 hundred, miles

1.17 some, cake

1.18 ten, hamburgers

1.19 no, papers

1.20 black, dog

1.21 Aunt, Jane, brick, house

1.22 pretty, flowers

1.23 Jim, sack, race

1.24 football, sunny, Saturdays

1.25 The yellow cat purred.

1.26 The big dog barked.

1.27 The race car went fast.

1.28 main

1.29 rotten

1.30 baby

1.31 long

1.32 lost

1.33–1.42 Examples:

1.33 nice

1.34 six, nice

1.35 pretty

1.36 pretty, little

1.37 red

1.38 big, red

1.39 big, red, brick

1.40 little

1.41 little, red

1.42 pretty, little, red

1.43 Any order:
a. how many
b. what kind
c. which one

1.44 a noun

1.45 Teacher check

1.46 Teacher check

1.47 Teacher check

1.48 bubble

1.49 castle

1.50 impossible

1.51 bundle

1.52 vegetable

1.53 invisible

1.54 saddle

1.55 needle

1.56 tremble

1.57 possible

1.58 bubble

1.59 impossible

1.60 tremble

1.61 castle

1.62 vegetable

1.63 invisible

1.64 Any order
a. saddle
b. impossible
c. tremble
d. needle
e. bubble
f. bundle
g. castle
h. possible

SELF TEST 1

1.01 a. 1
      b. 4
      c. 2
      d. 3
      e. 6
      f. 5

1.02 4, 1, 3, 2

1.03 <u>On the way home, we saw a deer beside the road. We got home just in time for school to start</u>.
Last summer, we went to visit Grandma and Grandpa. They live on a farm. We helped with some of the work. I helped gather the eggs. My brother helped haul the hay. All too soon, it was time to leave. On the way home, we saw a deer beside the road. We got home just in time for school to start.

1.04 Any order:
      a. person
      b. place
      c. thing
      d. time

1.05 Any order
      a. how many
      b. which one
      c. what kind

1.06 Examples:
      a. four
      b. several
      c. many

1.07 Examples:
      a. blue
      b. brick
      c. rainy

1.08 Examples:
      a. big
      b. baby
      c. left

1.09 (long)

1.010 (many)

1.011 (sour)

SECTION 2

2.1 a. cow
      b. black-and-white
      c. New Mexico State Fair
      d. Betty Jackson
      e. 16
      f. Clines Corners, New Mexico

2.2 blue

2.3 twelve

2.4 none

2.5 since it was a calf

2.6 Betty

2.7 a. ✓
      b.
      c. ✓
      d. ✓
      e.
      f.
      g.
      h. ✓
      i. ✓
      j. ✓
      k.
      l. ✓

2.8 a. Carmen
      b. takes her baby sister for a walk
      c. in the sunshine
      d. Mother is busy

2.9 Teacher check

2.10 a. Have a nice day.
      b. The Lord is my shepherd.

2.11 Teacher check

2.12 No, I cannot draw the crunch of the leaves. Words (adjectives) must be used to describe the crunch.

2.13 David, Saul

2.14 David, soldier

2.15 Goliath, David

2.16 Goliath, giant

2.17 Samson, lion

2.18 Samson, man

2.19 Any order:
older
bigger
stronger
faster

2.20   Any order:
younger
littler
weaker
slower
(not littlest)

2.21   Example:
Beauty is bigger and older than Star.

2.22   bigger
littler
harder
hardest
biggest
littlest

2.23   softer
bigger

2.24   Example:
Marshmallows are softer than the hard rocks.

2.25   Example:
Rocks are harder and warmer than snowballs.

2.26   a. busier
b. busiest

2.27   a. prettier
b. prettiest

2.28   a. dirtier
b. dirtiest

2.29   a. crazier
b. craziest

2.30   a. fancier
b. fanciest

2.31   a. steadier
b. steadiest

2.32   a. scarier
b. scariest

2.33   Example:
The boy is dirtier than the girl.

2.34   Example:
That pig is the dirtiest of all the pigs in the pen.

2.35   thin dim wet mad fat

2.36   a. thin, thinner, thinnest
b. dim, dimmer, dimmest
c. wet, wetter, wettest
d. mad, madder, maddest
e. fat, fatter, fattest

2.37   1. longer
2.38   2. braver
2.39   3. cleaner
2.40   4. brightest
2.41   5. strongest
2.42   6. biggest
2.43   7. nastiest
2.44   8. softest
2.45   9. highest
2.46   10. faster
2.47   11. higher
2.48   12. happier
2.49   13. prettiest
2.50   Teacher check
2.51   Teacher check
2.52   Teacher check
2.53   Teacher check
2.54   a. everyone
b. barnyard
c. gingerbread
d. cornfield
e. Somebody
f. upstairs
g. everyone
h. themselves
i. anyone
j. halfway
k. understand
l. gingerbread

2.55   a. anyway
b. anyone
c. halfway
d. upstairs
e. barnyard
f. sometime
g. understand
h. neighborhood

SELF TEST 2

2.01 Example:
We built a tree house.

2.02 backyard
tomorrow
leftover boards
big tree
last night
uncle

2.03 taller
2.04 funniest
2.05 dimmest
2.06 fattest
2.07 older
2.08 softer
2.09 longer
2.010 ~~People long ago had to get water from a well~~
~~in the city. David had many mighty men.~~

2.011 Examples:
tiny
soft
little
funny

2.012 Examples:
huge
angry
ugly
taller

2.013 thinner
oldest
seven
fattest
angrier
scary
pretty
ugly
clean
taller
brightest
funniest
softer
higher
biggest

2.014 T
2.015 T
2.016 NT
2.017 T
2.018 NT
2.019 NT
2.020 T

2.021 Example:
The old dog was slower than the puppy.

2.022 Example:
Two old, fat, angry men were chasing three
cute, black-and-white kittens.

SECTION 3

3.1   a. 5
     b. 2
     c. 3
     d. 4
     e. 1

3.2   Mother: "I hope your dad doesn't have to work very long this evening."

3.3   Mother: "I guess he must be one of the best electricians around."

3.4   Mother: "It's just our old hound dog, Rex."

3.5   Mother: "Look, he's already gone back to sleep and is beginning to snore again."

3.6   Millie: "He couldn't remember Daddy's name."

3.7   Mother: "Yes, there goes Rex down the road to greet him."

3.8   Any order:
     a. Mother—ranch wife; wife of an electrician at the mine
     b. Millie—nine-year-old girl; is learning how to make a quilt for sister's present
     c. Jenny—younger sister; 7 years old, also learning to quilt

3.9   Any order:
     a. Father
     b. Mr. Hood
     c. Rex, the dog

3.10 living room
     near a mining town
     rugs and lamps
     ranch house
     chairs and sofa
     front porch
     screen door

3.11 Teacher check
3.12 ran
3.13 sit
3.14 jump
3.15 flew
3.16 baked
3.17 called
3.18 smell
3.19 spilled
3.20 laughed
3.21 ride
3.22 sang
3.23 walk

3.24 found
3.25 ran
3.26 told
3.27 wash
3.28 plays
3.29 yelled
3.30 cried
3.31 walk
3.32 listens
3.33 drew
3.34 cleaned
3.35 read
3.36 are
3.37 were
3.38 were
3.39 is
3.40 are
3.41 am
3.42 was
3.43 had taken
3.44 have seen
3.45 will bake
3.46 has worn
3.47 can swim
3.48 would fix, would let
3.49 talked, laughed
3.50 walked, ran
3.51 ran, jumped
3.52 jump, count
3.53 mopped, dusted
3.54 started, drove
3.55 ran, helped
3.56 hurried, cleaned
3.57 Teacher check
3.58 Teacher check

3.59
a. arrive
b. fire
c. arrive
d. amaze
e. figure
f. decide
g. whisper
h. blink
i. beach
j. joy
k. escape
l. cheer
m. gaze
n. cheer
o. bother
p. match
q. deliver
r. exercise
s. escape
t. check
u. beach
v. figure
w. amaze
x. escape
y. cheer
z. bother

3.60 decide, bicycle, check, tire, start, cheer, arrive, blink, escape, whisper, gaze, minute, figure, laugh

SELF TEST 3

3.01 a play.

3.02 the plan or the main story.

3.03 the place where the play happens.

3.04 by the way the stage looks.

3.05 the people in the play.

3.06 ate

3.07 ran, jumped

3.08 swept, dusted

3.09 cleaned

3.010 baked, decorated

3.011 opened, crawled

3.012 walked

3.013 fell, hurt

3.014 fell, tore

3.015 was

3.016 was

3.017 are

3.018 am

3.019 is

3.020 were

3.021 will push

3.022 should cross

3.023 has crawled

3 024 has watched

3.025 will fix

3.026 will shine

3.027 had picked

3 028
a. 4
b. 1
c. 5
d. 3
e. 2

3.029 Samuel was a little boy in the Bible. At first, Samuel was too little to go to God's house. Samuel grew to be a bigger boy. Samuel's father and mother took him to God's house. Samuel was happy to live in God's house.

3.030 ~~Peggy liked her new shoes.~~

3.031 blue

3.032 funny

3.033 six

3.034 fried

3.035 black, white

3.036 bigger

3 037 prettiest

3.038 bravest

3.039 longer

LIFEPAC TEST

1. Our family had just moved into a new house.
2. This Sunday would be the first time to go to our new church.
3. I put on my good clothes and helped my little sister get dressed.
4. My family walked down the street together.
5. A nice man greeted us at the door.
6. The boys and girls were glad that I had come to their church.

7.–18. Examples:

7. four
8. many
9. eight
10. some
11. biggest
12. dirty
13. chocolate
14. happy
15. soft
16. loud
17. mean
18. green
19. taller
20. prettiest
21. strangest

22.–27. Examples:

22. He is black and white.
23. He has blue eyes.
24. His tail is short and stubby.
25. I got a blue dress from Mom and Daddy.
26. Grandma gave me a pink sweater.
27. Aunt Jane sent me some white socks.
28. T
29. T
30. NT
31. T
32. T
33. T
34. sit
35. laughed
36. catches
37. cross
38. has
39. will
40. was / am
41. have

ALTERNATE LIFEPAC TEST

1. Mother's birthday is coming up next Tuesday.
2. I had saved my money for a long time to buy a birthday present for her.
3. So, I asked Dad this morning if we could go to the store.
4. Dad took me to a bookstore.
5. We looked all around the bookstore.
6. We found a new Bible for Mother's birthday.

7.–18. Examples:

7. chocolate
8. smaller
9. happy
10. maple
11. orange
12. hard
13. noisy
14. funny
15. Some
16. two
17. few
18. hundred
19. Sentence to leave out:
   Shepherds take care of sheep.
20. a play
21. a writing that tells a person's thoughts
22. funniest
23. wiser
24. big

25.–28. Examples:

25. walked
26. read
27. makes
28. sing

SPELLING TEST

1	bubble	The water will **bubble** when it is hot.	bubble
2	bundle	**Bundle** up to keep warm.	bundle
3	impossible	Nothing is **impossible** with Jesus.	impossible
4	invisible	Many stars are **invisible** in the daytime.	invisible
5	needle	Tommy bought a new **needle** for his football.	needle
6	saddle	Mary learned to **saddle** her pony.	saddle
7	vegetable	Corn, peas, and carrots are in the **vegetable** group.	vegetable
8	anything	Is there **anything** special you want for your birthday?	anything
9	anywhere	We can go **anywhere** you wish for vacation.	anywhere
10	cornfield	We have a scarecrow in our **cornfield**.	cornfield
11	gingerbread	We made **gingerbread** houses for the fair.	gingerbread
12	neighborhood	A new family moved into our **neighborhood**.	neighborhood
13	sometime	Please clean your room **sometime** today.	sometime
14	themselves	They hurt **themselves** sledding down the hill.	themselves
15	understand	I do not **understand** the question.	understand
16	amaze	The story will **amaze** you when you hear it.	amaze
17	arrive	Melissa, what time did you **arrive** this morning?	arrive
18	blink	It is necessary to **blink** our eyes frequently.	blink
19	cheer	Let's stand up and **cheer** for our team.	cheer
20	decide	I couldn't **decide** which path to take.	decide
21	escape	Randy tried to **escape** from the swarm of bees.	escape
22	exercise	Running is great **exercise**.	exercise
23	figure	Lee made a perfect **figure** out of clay.	figure
24	gaze	When Paul reached the top of the hill he could **gaze** across the valley.	gaze
25	everyone	Is **everyone** allowed to go?	everyone

LANGUAGE ARTS 308

ALTERNATE LIFEPAC TEST

NAME _____

DATE _____

SCORE _____

22
28

Each answer = 1 point

Write these sentences in sequence.

So, I asked Dad this morning if we could go to the store.

Mother's birthday is coming up next Tuesday.

We found a new Bible for Mother's birthday there.

Dad took me to a bookstore.

I had saved my money for a long time to buy a birthday present for her.

We looked all around the bookstore.

1. _____

2. _____

3. _____

4. _____

5. _____

6. _____

orange	maple	two	happy
funny	some	chocolate	hundred
smaller	hard	few	noisy

Choose an adjective that tells *what kind* from the box to put in each sentence. Write it on the line.

7. I like to eat _____ cookies.

8. My little sister had _____ feet than I do.

9. Why are those people so _____ ?

10. Our swing is in the _____ tree.

Choose an adjective that tells *which one* from the box and write it on the line in each sentence.

11. Bring me that _____ book.

12. This is a _____ rock to site on.

13. Our dog is not a _____ dog to the neighbors.

14. Where did you get that _____ story?

Choose an adjective that tells *how many* from the box and write it in the correct sentence.

15. _____ boys and girls are in the race.

16. I see only _____ people on the slide.

17. May I have a _____ grapes?

18. This highway is a _____ miles long.

Rewrite this story, leaving out the detail that does not go with the main idea.

19. God gave us a great gift. One night long ago, a light shone brightly. Shepherds saw angels who told them where to find God's gift. Shepherds take care of sheep. They went to Bethlehem and found God's gift. It was His son, Jesus.

_____

_____

_____

_____

_____

Complete these sentences.

20. A drama is _____ .

21. An essay is _____ .

Choose an adjective which *compares* **from the box to complete each sentence.**

wise	big	funny
wiser	bigger	funnier
wisest	biggest	funniest

22. I think that's the _____ story I've heard.

23. After the accident, Tom was a _____ person.

24. What a _____ airplane the SST is!

Think of a verb for each sentence. Write it on the line.

25. Jesus _____ across the water to the fishermen's boat.

26. Do you _____ books every night?

27. My mom _____ the best cakes.

28. I can _____ all by myself.

ALTERNATE SPELLING TEST

1	castle	The **castle** was built on a hill.	castle
2	possible	At night, it is **possible** to see many stars.	possible
3	tremble	The loud noise made my puppy **tremble**.	tremble
4	anyone	I do not know **anyone** here.	anyone
5	anyway	I did not want to go **anyway**.	anyway
6	barnyard	The chickens are in the **barnyard**.	barnyard
7	halfway	I will meet you **halfway** down the street.	halfway
8	somebody	**Somebody** fell down in the race.	somebody
9	upstairs	Ivan will meet you **upstairs**.	upstairs
10	amaze	The story will **amaze** you when you hear it.	amaze
11	beach	David was so happy to be going to the **beach** with his family.	beach
12	bother	You should not **bother** a friend when he is studying.	bother
13	check	Kristopher, please **check** your name off my list.	check
14	decide	I couldn't **decide** which path to take.	decide
15	exercise	Running is great **exercise**.	exercise
16	gaze	When Paul reached the top of the hill, he could **gaze** across the valley.	gaze
17	match	Let's go to the tennis **match** today.	match
18	impossible	Nothing is **impossible** with Jesus.	impossible
19	vegetable	Corn, peas, and carrots are in the **vegetable** group.	vegetable
20	gingerbread	We made **gingerbread** houses for the fair.	gingerbread
21	neighborhood	A new family moved into our **neighborhood**.	neighborhood
22	themselves	They hurt **themselves** sledding down the hill.	themselves
23	invisible	Many stars are **invisible** in the daytime.	invisible
24	deliver	Our postman did not **deliver** the correct package.	deliver
25	fry	Would you like to help Mom **fry** the chicken?	fry

LANGUAGE ARTS 309

Unit 9: More Reading and Writing

TEACHER NOTES

MATERIALS NEEDED FOR LIFEPAC	
Required	Suggested
None	• photocopies of Book Report Form • exposed film or transparencies

ADDITIONAL LEARNING ACTIVITIES

Section 1: Grouping Information

1. Discuss these questions with your class.

    a. What does *classify* mean?

    b. Do you know how to classify?

    c. In what way do we classify our things in the classroom?

    d. What is an adverb?

    e. What do adverbs do? What do adverbs tell?

    f. Can you make a sentence using these adverbs: *fast*, *quickly*, *now*, and so forth?

2. Have all students stand. Let one student classify the others by such things as brown shoes, girls and boys, tall and short, blue-eyed; and so forth.

3. After viewing an educational video about classifying, discuss the way things are classified.

4. Have students take turns (as in charades) to "show" an adverb. Allow others to guess.

5. Have students view an educational video on adverbs.

6. Have students bring collection of leaves, rocks, and so forth. On a large cardboard, classify them and mount them for display.

7. Have students find pictures of animals in magazines, cut them out, and paste them on paper to indicate classification.

8. Have students write prefixes *un-*, *re-*, and *dis-* on the top of a page. Find as many words as possible to put under each heading.

Section 2: Finding Information

1. Discuss these questions with your class.

    a. What is information?

    b. Why do we need information?

    c. Where can we find the information we need?

    d. What are the parts of a thank-you letter?

    e. What punctuation and capitalization do we use in the greeting of a letter? in the body? in the closing? in the signature?

2. Have students make a list of words with suffixes *-ful*, *-less*, or *-ness*. Choose those that will characterize their attitudes and actions during the rest of that school day. Check with them the next morning to see how well each one did.

3. Write the names for the parts of a thank-you letter on 3" x 5" cards. Write a sample of each part on 3" x 5" cards. Put the cards in a large box in the middle of a circle of students. At a given signal, the students will crawl to the box and find a card with the name of the part of the letter to match the sample each has been given. The first person to crawl to his own seat with matching cards will be called the winner.

4. Write the suffixes *-ful*, *-ness*, and *-less* on enough papers for half the class. Write root words on papers for the others. Pin the papers on the backs of the students. They must find a partner.

5. Each person makes up a situation that would call for a thank-you letter. Then, they can exchange situations. Each writes a thank-you letter correctly.

6. When the class visits the zoo or a bakery or whatever, be sure to have each student write a thank-you letter.

Section 3: Guessing the Ending

1. Discuss these questions with your class.

   a. Can you name two kinds of book reports?

   b. What does the suffix *-teen* mean?

   c. Can you name some words with the suffix *-teen*?

2. Find a quiet place for a pair of students. Let them take turns reading aloud. They will need to choose a book that both of them will enjoy.

3. Compile a book report book. Ask each student to illustrate each book report made. Staple the books together and use wallpaper for a book cover.

4. Encourage volunteers to read aloud to the group at story time or to younger children at their story time.

Administer the LIFEPAC Spelling Test.

> The test is provided in this Teacher's Guide.
> Evaluate the tests and review the words the students spelled incorrectly.
> If necessary, review all of the words in the unit to prepare for the alternate spelling test.
> Administer the Alternate LIFEPAC Spelling test that is provided in this Teacher's Guide.

Administer the LIFEPAC Test.

> The test is to be administered in one session. Give no help except with directions.
> Evaluate the tests and review areas where the students have done poorly.
> Review the pages and activities that stress the concepts tested.
> If necessary, administer the Alternate LIFEPAC Test.

ANSWER KEYS

SECTION 1

1.1   car
1.2   fork
1.3   sun
1.4   plate
1.5   potato
1.6   a. July
         b. table
         c. Dad
         d. Christmas
         e. lunch
1.7   Any order:
         Ride In
         car
         train
         wagon
         truck
         airplane
         Swim In
         pool
         river
         ocean
         pond
         lake
         Sleep In
         pajamas
         tent
         crib
         nightgown
         bed
1.8   My little brother can run fast.
1.9   Kathy ran happily up the sidewalk.
1.10 The boys and girls were sitting quietly.
1.11 Bob answered all the questions correctly.
1.12 Does Jack paint well?
1.13 You must always play safely.
1.14 Grandpa cheerfully does his work.
1.15 Suzie hit the ball hard.
1.16 The children sang joyfully
1.17 We looked everywhere for our caps.
1.18 Will you please sit down?
1.19 We saw the hot air balloon go up.
1.20 Please put the book there.
1.21 Will you bring the chair here?
1.22 We plan to go away for the whole summer.
1.23 how; quietly
1 24 how; joyfully
1.25 how; well
1.26 how; closely

1.27 where; down
1.28 where; anywhere
1.29 how; differently
1.30 how; sadly
1.31 where; here
1.32 An adverb is a word that limits or adds to the meaning of the verb.
1.33 Teacher check
1.34 Teacher check
1.35 Teacher check
1.36 Teacher check
1.37 Teacher check
1.38 Teacher check
1.39 Teacher check
1.40 a. unfasten
         b. dishonor
         c. disappoint
         d. dislike
         e. refold
         f. unbent
         g. unhappy
         h. disappear
         i. refigure
         j. untie
         k. disband
         l. reload
         m. recheck
         n. remodel
         o. uncover
1.41 Mix Up
         a. tie
         b. honor
         c. check
         d. load
         e. happy
         f. model
         g. fasten
         h. appear
         Fix Up
         a. untie
         b. dishonor
         c. recheck
         d. reload
         e. unhappy
         f. remodel
         g. unfasten
         h. disappear

SELF TEST 1

1.01 Animals
cat
dog
horse
snake
chicken
People
girl
grandmother
mother
boy
aunt
Plants
weeds
grass
bush
tree
flower

1.02 a. ~~water~~
b. ~~ice cube~~
c. ~~sister~~
d. ~~yesterday~~
e. ~~Easter~~

1.03 You should play safely

1.04 Good students work carefully

1.05 Sometimes, God speaks quietly within us.

1.06 We looked everywhere for the library book.

1.07 I can hit the ball hard.

1.08 Please answer carefully.

1.09 Put the chair here.

1.010 Does your mother paint well?

1.011 Please sit quietly.

1.012 Joseph walked slowly.

1.013 how

1.014 where

1.015 how

1.016 how

1.017 where

1.018 how

1.019 how

1.020 how

SECTION 2

2.1 that which is called out

2.2 a small, large, or worldwide religious body

2.3 The followers of Jesus got together in groups.

2.4 Saint Paul's Epistles

2.5 yes

2.6 The people in those churches are followers of Jesus Christ.

2.7 no

2.8 360 S. River Drive
San Rafael, CA 94902
April 26, 2016

2.9 Example:
526 N. 15th Ave.
Phoenix, AZ 85031
April 27, 2016

2.10 Example:
Dear Grandma,

2.11 Dear Uncle Joe,

2.12 Teacher check

2.13 Example:
Love,
name

2.14 Teacher check

2.15 Teacher check

2.16 Teacher check

2.17 Teacher check

2.18 Teacher check

2.19 Teacher check

2.20 Teacher check

2.21 Examples:
a. Mr. Jones has his own trucking business.
b. Knowing God brings happiness.
c. There is a crispness in the morning air.
d. The aimless wheel rolled down the hill.
e. It is needless to say, but you are beautiful.
f. My baby brother is helpless.
g. Make yourself useful and answer the telephone.
h. Don't be fearful but trust God.

2.22 dark   ful
care   less
sleep   ness
cloud
cheer
good
Any order:
careful or careless
sleepless
darkness
cloudless
cheerful
goodness

2.23   Across
1. fearful
2. happiness
3. sleepless
4. careful
5. goodness
6. crispness
Down
7. aimless
8. helpless
9. handful
10. useful
11. cheerful
12. darkness

SELF TEST 2

2.01   Any order:
a. heading
b. greeting
c. body
d. closing
e. signature

2.02   a. 1334 E. Ann Arbor St.
b. Silver City, NM
c. April 6, 2016

2.03   Dear Aunt Judy,

2.04   Example:
Your granddaughter, Ann

2.05   special facts about something or facts

2.06   to find out special things about something—to learn

2.07   encyclopedia

2.08   science book

2.09   Bible Men
Any order:
Paul
David
Moses
Samuel
Bible Books
Any order:
Acts
Genesis
Romans
Psalms
Samuel

2.010 Please play carefully

2.011 Tom's mother kicked the ball hard

2.012 Boys and girls walk quietly

2.013 The baby cried loudly

2.014 The boys and girls laughed happily

SECTION 3

3.1   Teacher check
3.2   Examples:
       Billy's dad didn't see the bicycle and backed
       over it.
       or
       Billy's dad backed over the bicycle.
3.3   Examples:
       made Jane scrub the cat with tomato juice
       or made the cat go away
3.4   atlas
3.5   encyclopedia
3.6   dictionary
3.7   dictionary
3.8   encyclopedia
3.9   encyclopedia
3.10   a. maid
       b. meat
       c. mice
       d. mountain
       e. mule
3.11   a. school
       b. shell
       c. slip
       d. sneeze
       e. sunburn
3.12   a. C
       b. B
       c. M
       d. N
       e. X-Y-Z
       f. X-Y-Z
3.13   Teacher check
3.14   Teacher check
3.15   Teacher check
3.16   Teacher check
3.17   Any order:
       a. sixteen
       b. fourteen
       c. seventeen
       d. thirteen
       e. nineteen
       f. fifteen
       g. eighteen

3.18   fourteen or favorite
       familiar
       favorite or fourteen
       fifteen
       famous
3.19   B
       beginning
        C
       comfortable
       complete
        E
       eighteen
       enormous
       experiment
        F
       familiar
       famous
       favorite
       fifteen
       fourteen
        N
       nineteen
        T
       thirteen
        S
       seventeen
       sixteen
3.20   comfortable
3.21   seventeen, eighteen, fourteen, thirteen,
       nineteen, sixteen, *or* fifteen
3.22   nineteen
3.23   favorite
3.24   complete
3.25   famous
3.26   thirteen
3.27   enormous
3.28   seventeen
3.29   beginning

SELF TEST 3

3.01   atlas
3.02   dictionary
3.03   encyclopedia
3.04   dictionary
3.05   atlas or encyclopedia
3.06   dictionary
3.07   encyclopedia
3.08   dictionary
3.09   encyclopedia
3.010 dictionary
3.011–3.020 Examples:
3.011 you stay home from school
3.012 you are not hungry
3.013 makes them for you
3.014 bring kids to school
3.015 be disappointed
3.016 help you solve your problem
3.017 have to walk
3.018 good grades
3.019 play well or win
3.020 get a star or do well
3.021 where
      a. here
      b. there
      c. down
      d. away
      how
      e. slowly
      f. loudly
      g. fast
      h. sweetly
3.022 I can run fast.
3.023 The sun shone brightly
3.024 The boys and girls lined up quickly
3.025 The class sat quietly
3.026 Any order:
      a. heading
      b. greeting
      c. body
      d. closing
      e. signature
3.027 Any order:
      a. name of book
      b. author
      c. illustrator
      d. something about the book
      e. why you did or did not like the book
      or number of pages

LIFEPAC TEST

1. Time
   Any order:
   a. Saturday
   b. yesterday
   c. an hour
   Place
   Any order:
   d. school
   e. home
   f. church
   Activity
   Any order:
   g. football
   h. soccer
   i. running
2. The horse is running slowly.
3. The ball came down.
4. Quickly, get your camera!
5. The children can stand up quietly.
6. Please bring your coat here.
7. Golden Richards can run fast.
8. facts about something
9. to find out about a subject
10. 5622 N. Street
    Bakersfield, CA
    April, 2, 2016
11. Example: Dear Aunt,
12. Example: Love,
13. Example: Patsy
14.–19. Examples:
14. will not be fun
15. try to be quiet
16. answer her
17. will clean and bandage it
18. answer you
19. get good grades
20. encyclopedia or atlas
21. dictionary or encyclopedia
22. atlas or encyclopedia
23. dictionary or encyclopedia
24. atlas
25. dictionary
26. dictionary or encyclopedia
27. encyclopedia
28. Either order:
    a. written
    b. oral

ALTERNATE LIFEPAC TEST

1.–5. Any order:
1. giraffe
2. building
3. tree
4. church
5. giant
6.–10. Any order:
6. ant
7. turtle
8. grass
9. doghouse
10. baby
11. butter
12. village
13. shovel
14. fast
15. quickly
16. there
17. down
18. loudly
19. bird
20. seven inches long
21. yellowish brown
22. tall grass or clover fields
23. four to seven
24. Any order:
    heading
    greeting
    body
    closing
    signature
25. Any order:
    author's name
    illustrator's name
    title
    something about the book
    why you did
    or did not like it
26.–29. Examples:
26. flood
27. probably smile back
28. take care of it
29. learn

SPELLING TEST

1	disappear	The clouds made the sun **disappear**.	disappear
2	disappoint	Charlie did not mean to **disappoint** you.	disappoint
3	disband	The choir will **disband** for summer vacation.	disband
4	dishonor	Never **dishonor** your parents.	dishonor
5	dislike	I **dislike** spinach even though it is good for me.	dislike
6	recheck	Uncle Joe will **recheck** his gas mileage.	recheck
7	refigure	The bank will **refigure** the numbers.	refigure
8	refold	Mom had to **refold** the clothes after Tommy knocked them over.	refold
9	reload	I helped mom **reload** the dishwasher.	reload
10	remodel	The men will **remodel** the office tomorrow.	remodel
11	unbent	Father **unbent** my bicycle spokes.	unbent
12	uncover	Now that the weather is warmer, we can **uncover** the tomatoes.	uncover
13	unfasten	**Unfasten** the line from the boat.	unfasten
14	unhappy	Shawn was **unhappy** when the trip was cancelled.	unhappy
15	untie	It is easier to **untie** my shoes than tie them.	untie
16	aimless	The speaker was **aimless** in his thoughts.	aimless
17	business	The man presented a **business** card to the secretary.	business
18	careful	Our teacher tells us to be **careful** when crossing the street.	careful
19	cheerful	Molly is such a **cheerful** girl.	cheerful
20	cloudless	The birds soared through the **cloudless** blue sky.	cloudless
21	crispness	The **crispness** of the mountain air brings back many memories.	crispness
22	darkness	**Darkness** comes quickly in the mountains.	darkness
23	fearful	I was **fearful** when the huge black bear saw me.	fearful
24	goodness	Do you remember the song that goes "Surely **goodness** and mercy shall follow me"?	goodness
25	handful	I ate a whole **handful** of wild blackberries.	handful

LANGUAGE ARTS 309

ALTERNATE LIFEPAC TEST

NAME _____

DATE _____

SCORE _____

Each answer = 1 point

Put the word from the box in the right classification.

giraffe	turtle	church	building	tree
doghouse	ant	grass	giant	baby

Tall

1. _____

2. _____

3. _____

4. _____

5. _____

Short

6. _____

7. _____

8. _____

9. _____

10. _____

Put a circle around the word in each group that does not belong with the classification.

11. brown
red
orange
butter

12. Dutch
English
Spanish
village

13. broom
sweeper
shovel
dust rag

Put a circle around the adverb in each sentence.

14. Bill can run fast.

15. Mary quickly called the fire department.

16. Put that pencil there.

17. We saw the big jet come down.

18. The little boy banged loudly on his drum.

Read this paragraph to get information. Then answer the questions below.

BOBOLINK. The bobolink is a bird in the family of black birds or orioles. The bobolink sings a lovely song. The bird is about seven inches long. Both the male and the female are colored with a yellowish brown with a lighter color underneath. Bobolinks fly north in summer as far as Canada. They return to the United States to build nests in tall grass or clover fields. The mother bird usually lays four to seven eggs.

19. What is a bobolink? _____

20. How big is a bobolink? _____

21. What color are bobolinks? _____

22. Where do they nest? _____

23. How many eggs does the mother bird lay? _____

Do these activities.

24. Name the five parts of a thank-you letter.

_____

_____

_____

_____

_____

25. What are five things to include in a book report?

_____

_____

_____

_____

_____

Complete these sentences.

26. If it rains very, very hard, the water in the river will _____ .

27. If you smile at others, they will _____ .

28 If you have a pet, you will have to _____ .

29. If you study hard, you will _____ .

ALTERNATE SPELLING TEST

1	happiness	My **happiness** comes from the Lord Jesus.	happiness
2	helpless	The **helpless** animals were rescued by a fireman.	helpless
3	needles	Dry pine **needles** will start a fire very easily.	needles
4	sleepless	Parents spend many **sleepless** nights caring for their young children.	sleepless
5	useful	My Bible is very **useful** in church.	useful
6	beginning	In the **beginning**, God created the heavens and the earth.	beginning
7	comfortable	My sleeping bag is as **comfortable** as my bed.	comfortable
8	complete	I want to **complete** my model before we go.	complete
9	eighteen	The farmer harvested **eighteen** dozen bushels of apples.	eighteen
10	enormous	The **enormous** banana split had three scoops of ice cream and lots of whipped cream.	enormous
11	experiment	Be careful when you do any **experiment**.	experiment
12	familiar	The **familiar** hills soon came into view.	familiar
13	famous	The most **famous** book in the world is the Bible.	famous
14	favorite	My **favorite** fishing spot is a creek south of town.	favorite
15	fifteen	We counted **fifteen** deer in the herd.	fifteen
16	fourteen	My parents were married **fourteen** years ago.	fourteen
17	nineteen	**Nineteen** years ago, a severe earthquake struck.	nineteen
18	seventeen	We saw **seventeen** crocodiles at the zoo.	seventeen
19	sixteen	The boat stalled **sixteen** times while we were water skiing.	sixteen
20	thirteen	The mother rabbit had **thirteen** babies.	thirteen
21	untie	It is easier to **untie** my shoes than tie them.	untie
22	aimless	The speaker was **aimless** in his thoughts.	aimless
23	business	The man presented a **business** card to the secretary.	business
24	careful	Our teacher tells us to be **careful** when crossing the street.	careful
25	cheerful	Molly is such a **cheerful** girl.	cheerful

LANGUAGE ARTS 310

Unit 10: Looking Back

TEACHER NOTES

MATERIALS NEEDED FOR LIFEPAC	
Required	Suggested
None	• tagboard • newsprint (for maps) • atlas • encyclopedia • dictionary • banner paper

ADDITIONAL LEARNING ACTIVITIES

Section 1: Review Sequencing and Context Clues

1. Discuss these questions with your class.

   a. What do we mean by using context clues?

   b. How do we mark a long vowel? a short vowel?

   c. How can you tell if a group of words is a sentence?

   d. What do we put at the end of a sentence?

   e. What kind of sentence do we use each of the marks for?

2. Have each student write his name: last name, comma, then first name on a piece of construction paper. Be sure to leave space on each end. It may be decorated in any way the student desires. Then, have the first person in alphabetical order come to the front of the room. The second person then comes and they cut the ends of their paper to resemble pieces of a puzzle. Continue until each person has had a turn. Display the puzzle around the room.

3. Cut comic strips apart. Mount on tagboard and laminate. Put them in envelopes. Have students put them together in sequence.

4. Ask each student to make a game: Fold paper into sixteen squares. In each square, write one of the words below. Be sure to mix them up. Then, have the children cut sixteen markers from scraps of construction paper (they must cover the square). Teacher makes two sets of 4" x 6" cards with long a, long e, long i, long o, long u, short a, short e, short i, short o, short u, r-controlled, and rule breaker. Teacher shows cards one at a time and if the student has a word showing the rule, he covers it with a marker. First person to have four in a row is the winner. (To make it harder, winner must have all words covered.)

bread	fork	cause	seven	tray
pin	break	land	geese	slide
mule	suit	eight	nurse	drum
march	cue	tub	flag	order

   (These words may be changed and the game played many times.)

5. Have student pairs make up riddles. Put them on writing paper: I am a big animal. I start with the letter e. I have a big trunk. What am I? Exchange paper and write the answers.

6. Each student in the pair writes a short story, or copies one from a book. Each sentence is written on a 3" x 5" card. Exchange cards and put the story in sequence.

Section 2: Review Maps

1. Discuss these questions with your class.

    a. Do you know how to read a map?

    b. What are symbols?

    c. Why do we use symbols?

    d. What is the key on a map?

    e. How do you tell directions on a map?

    f. Can you follow directions? Put your hands on your head; on your shoulders; on your cheeks; on your back; on your knees.

    g. Can you tell the rules for use of capital letters, periods, commas, question marks, and exclamation marks?

2. Play Simple Simon or Follow the Leader as exercise in following directions.

3. Have a spelling bee. Use spelling words in Sections I and II. If the students need more of a challenge, use spelling words from all the LIFEPACs.

4. Have pairs of students work on making charts for the classroom: Assign the subject, capitalization, periods, commas, and so on. Have the pairs paint the lettering and illustrations. Display the charts in the classroom.

5. Have student pairs study spelling words together. One student gives the word and the other spells it orally or on paper. Then exchange places and repeat.

6. Make a map of an imaginary town called Big Mud. Name the streets and locate the school, the church, the post office, the park, and the highway. Trace the route of the Fourth of July parade.

7. Make a map showing the course of a river with bridges, towns, highways, farmlands, or pastures along it. Students may use this map as a guide for making a model in clay of the river. Label the various parts and name the river.

8. Ask students to write Haiku or poetry. Display them on a "poem" bulletin board.

9. Give each student a "Follow Directions" sheet that has been photocopied.

    1. READ ALL DIRECTIONS BEFORE YOU DO ANYTHING.

    2. Put your name at the top of the paper, last name first.

    3. Write today's date under your name.

    4. Make a star in the upper left hand corner.

    5. Stand up by your desk and count to 100.

    6. Turn around three times before sitting down.

    7.-9. Make more directions.

    10. Do not do anything after you have read these instructions. Sit quietly, and watch what other students do.

10. Make a word-find puzzle like the one in this section with names of states or countries or use the spelling words.

11. Practice writing a tongue twister.
    Example: But Barry bounced the ball backwards breaking both bat and beads.

Section 3: Review Cause and Effect

1. Discuss these questions with your class.

    a. Can you describe a clarinet?

    b. When can students begin music lessons?

    c. Would you like to play in the band? what instrument?

    d. What are private music lessons? Do you pay for them?

    e. What do we mean by main idea? by supporting details? by cause and effect?

    f. What is a noun? an adjective? a verb? an adverb?

    g. What does each one (noun, verb, adjective, adverb) do in a sentence?

    h. What are helping words?

    i. Can you name the helping words?

    j. Why do we have helping verbs?

    k. What are the parts of a thank-you letter?

    l. What are silent letters in words? What are the most common silent letters?

2. Make lists either on the board or on chart paper of nouns, verbs, adjectives, and adverbs. Ask students to name them as you write them. Then pass writing paper and ask students to write a noun-verb sentence from the words on the lists. Keep adding adjectives and adverbs until you have the longest sentence you can make that is sensible. Continue by choosing another noun-verb sentence.

3. Have students make puppets. Draw a figure on paper and glue it to a popsicle stick. Make cloth puppets by sewing a round shape from muslin and marking features with a felt tip pen. Then students make up situations showing cause and effect.

4. Silent Letter Bounce: Place students in circles of six or eight students. Give one person a playground ball. He says the name of a silent w (wrap) or silent k word (knock) as he bounces the ball to another. The person who catches the ball spells the word and then says another word as he bounces the ball to another student. Continue in this manner for a limited number of minutes.

5. Write the main idea and give details of the story of Joseph and his coat of many colors (Genesis 37:2-4, 11, and 28) or the story of Peter's escape from prison (Acts 12:1-11).

6. Write letters to your Sunday school teacher inviting him or her to Sunday dinner at your home, your grandparents telling them about your new pet, or your parents explaining the schedule for the Christmas program.

7. Have students write as many details as they can about a picture poster that has been displayed.

8. Have each student cut from an old magazine pictures that show nouns. They may cut four and paste them at the top of four columns on a piece of paper. Write adjectives to describe the picture at the top.

9. Each student writes an original main idea. He passes his paper to next person who adds a detail and passes the paper on to next person who adds another detail, and so on. When the paper returns to the original author, he rewrites in sequence and in cursive hand-writing. These stories may be posted on the bulletin board.

Section 4: Review Fiction and Nonfiction

1. Discuss these questions with your class.

    a. Do you like to play baseball?

    b. How many people are on each team?

    c. Can you describe how baseball is played?

    d. Do any of you belong to a Little League team? a church team?

    e. How did baseball get started?

    f. What is recreational reading?

    g. What is reference reading?

    h. What is fiction?

    i. What is nonfiction?

    j. What is an atlas? an encyclopedia?

    k. Can you tell about a reference book you have used?

2. Ask each student to bring a large grocery bag. Cut the bag into a jacket by cutting a front on a wide side, a neck opening in the bottom, and arm holes in the side. On the back, have him make a "book jacket" of any of his favorite fiction readings. Allow students to wear them.

3. Have class make a book marker. Give each student a piece of felt about six inches long and one and a half inches wide. Have them decorate them with scraps of lace or other material. They may use glue or sew them. The bottom of the bookmark may be fringed by making snips in the felt.

4. Give pairs of students big pieces of banner paper. Fold the paper in half. On one side, make an illustration of a book that would be fiction and on the other side make an illustration of a nonfiction book. These may be painted with poster or tempera paint.

5. Have student pairs make jigsaw puzzles. Students draw a map, fiction picture, or nonfiction picture. Mount the picture on tagboard or cardboard. Teacher may then have it laminated. Cut the picture into good sized puzzle pieces. Exchange and work the puzzles. These may be stored in large envelopes.

6. Have students work in pairs to make a school atlas. They will make maps of the classroom, cafeteria, office, nurse's office, library, and so forth, on 9" x 12" drawing paper. When completed, put them together with a cardboard covered with wallpaper for the cover.

7. On 4" x 6" cards, write a subject for which students must find information and the definition. Let students choose a card and find the information in an encyclopedia; copy on a piece of paper. Return the card and choose another as time permits.

8. Have students go on a Scavenger Hunt or Discovery Trip. Photocopy written information to find either in the library or classroom. Examples:

    a. Find a good camping site for you family.

    b. What kind of music did Brahms write?

    c. Where did the English language come from?

    d. Find a new song that you do not know.

    e. What does the word potassium mean?

    f. What is a canine?

9. Have students make "comic strips." Divide a drawing paper into sections. Draw the pictures and write the conversations in the sections. Remind students that comics are usually fiction.

10. Have students bring small boxes and make a diorama of a nonfiction subject: Washington crossing the Delaware, Paul Revere's Ride, Betsy Ross and the Flag, Statue of Liberty, sports figures, and so forth. Make figures of stiff paper and make tabs on the bottom so that they will stand.

11. Using an atlas, calculate the miles between cities in adjoining states.

12. Read Genesis 22:1-14. Tell the story of Abraham's obedience to God in your own words.

Administer the LIFEPAC Spelling Test.

The test is provided in this Teacher's Guide.
Evaluate the tests and review the words the students spelled incorrectly.
If necessary, review all of the words in the unit to prepare for the alternate spelling test.
Administer the Alternate LIFEPAC Spelling test that is provided in this Teacher's Guide.

Administer the LIFEPAC Test.

The test is to be administered in one session. Give no help except with directions.
Evaluate the tests and review areas where the students have done poorly.
Review the pages and activities that stress the concepts tested.
If necessary, administer the Alternate LIFEPAC Test.

ANSWER KEYS

SECTION 1

1.1   a. x 4
        b. 1
        c. 2
        d. 3

1.2   a. 2
        b. 7
        c. 5
        d. 3
        e. 6

1.3   a. First, Jane puts a tablecloth on the table.
        b. Next, she puts on six plates.
        c. After she puts on the plates, Jane puts on the knives, forks, and spoons.
        d. Finally, the glasses go on.
        e. Now the table is ready.

1.4   take charge of
1.5   kept on
1.6   deeply, sound
1.7   not asleep
1.8   a. 1 flăg
        b. 1 pĭn
        c. 3 bāke
        d. 1 căb
        e. 3 lāke
        f. 1 tŭb
        g. 3 mūle
        h. 3 sāil
        i. 2 pāper
        j. 2 rōbŏt
        k. 3 gēese
        l. 3 cāne
        m. 1 hătch
        n. 3 bōat
        o. 1 sĕvĕn
        p. 1 ŏftĕn
        q. x weigh
        r. 1 drŭm
        s. 3 slīde
        t. 1 shrŭb
        u. 3 cŭe
        v. 3 tīe

1.9   cane
1.10 bed
1.11 cot
1.12 paste
1.13 ran
1.14 mean
1.15 seal
1.16 cube
1.17 fine

1.18 twine
1.19 ~~At the post office.~~
1.20 ~~Running home.~~
1.21 is a sentence
1.22 is a sentence
1.23 ~~Are here.~~
1.24 Where are you going?
1.25 I am going home.
1.26 My sister is four years old today.
1.27 Watch out!
1.28 What do you have in your sack?
1.29 We had fun at your house.
1.30 Mother, may I go see Grandma?
1.31 What time is school over?
1.32 The sky is falling!
1.33 Teacher check;
         Check for beginning capital letter, ending punctuation mark, and neat handwriting. One sentence has to be a question.
1.34 Any order:
         a. knee
         b. knock
         c. fight
         d. night
         e. wrong
         f. write
1.35 Any order:
         a. bēach
         b. spēak
         c. māid
         d. gōat
         e. spēech
         f. flōat
1.36 Either order:
         a. herd
         b. perfect
         Any order:
         c. nurse
         d. hurry
         e. circle
         Any order:
         f. cartoon
         g. apart
         h. guard
1.37 Any order:
         a. cartoon
         b. apart
         c. guard
1.38 Teacher check

SELF TEST 1

1.01 a. First, Ann pointed to the big book on the table.
 b. Ann asked Grandmother what the book was.
 c. Grandmother told her it was the Bible.
 d. Then, Grandmother picked up the Bible.
 e. Grandmother opened the Bible and read to Ann.

1.02 always shows love

1.03 money

1.04 sound

1.05 quiet

1.06 wild animals

1.07 a. mīne
 b. fĭt
 c. Frīdāy
 d. că̆bĭn
 e. frē̆ēze
 f. wē

1.08 Today is my birthday.

1.09 ~~nine years old~~

1.010 What time is it?

1.011 We have fun at school.

1.012 God answers our prayers.

1.013 ~~at suppertime~~

1.014 I had fun at school today.

1.015 Danger, watch out!

SECTION 2

2.1 Examples:
 a. Go east on the sidewalk to the third wing, turn south, and walk to the fourth room.
 b. Go west on the sidewalk to the third wing, turn south, and walk to the fourth room.
 c. Go east to the fourth wing and go south to the last room.

2.2 Teacher check

2.3 Sunday

2.4 Jesus

2.5 Wednesday

2.6 Capitalize

2.7 map skills

2.8 My Uncle John grows corn, wheat, and hay on his farm.

2.9 Mary, what do you want for dinner?

2.10 Yes, you may play basketball.

2.11 Jack, what time will Bill, Tom, and Sam get here?

2.12 Did you know I came from Dayton, Ohio?

2.13 I was born on March 2, 2008.

2.14 Today is Thursday, June 5, 2016.

2.15 We have red, green, blue, or yellow paper.

2.16 My parents visited Joplin, Missouri.

2.17 Jack, watch out!

2.18 Tom, please send this box to Las Cruces, New Mexico.

2.19 Teacher check:
 Sentences should use commas.
 One exclamation sentence needs to be included. Sentences should use periods and question marks.

2.20 M, M, T
 My aunt lives in Memphis, Tennessee.

2.21 M, I, L, S
 My sister and I attend Lincoln School.

2.22 T, F, M
 Today is Friday, May 6, 2016.

2.23 A, J, T, C
 Aunt Janie will he here on Thursday for Christmas.

2.24 I, T, R
 I have a cat named Tabby and a dog named Ruffian.

2.25 I, Y, N, P
 I'd like to visit Yellowstone National Park.

2.26 U, B, D
 Uncle Bob will take us to Disneyland.

2.27 M, J, G
 Mr. Jones prays to God every day.

2.28 b, d, e, g, i, j, k, l, o

2.29   Teacher check
2.30   Teacher check
2.31   a.   thrown
               grown
           b.   bright
               sight
               bicycle
           c.   leaves
               receive
               ceiling
               neither
           d.   vacation
               station
               direction
           e.   frown
           f.   candy
               everybody
               bicycle
2.32   a.   calf, calves
           b.   leaf, leaves
2.33   change the *f* to *v* and add *es*
           or drop the *f* and add *ves*
2.34   Teacher check

SELF TEST 2

2.01   north
2.02   west
2.03   go north
2.04   go east
2.05   go south
2.06   Mediterranean
2.07   Bashan
2.08   by the Jordan River
2.09   Mediterranean Sea
2.010   Dead Sea
2.011   a, b, d, e, f, h, i, j, l, m, n, p, q, s, t
2.012   ⓜy neighbor is ⓜr. ⓝickelson.
2.013   ⓒan you go to ⓐunt ⓢue's house on ⓣuesday?
2.014   ⓘ live at 647 ⓝorth ⓟleasant ⓢt.
2.015   ⓒ. ⓙ. ⓢmith lives in ⓓayton, ⓞhio.
2.016   ⓖrandma put a sandwich, an apple, three cookies, and some milk in my lunch.
2.017   ⓨes, your library book is due ⓕriday, ⓐug. 20, 2016.
2.018   ⓜary, will you watch ⓙoey?
2.019   a.   mīle
           b.   bĭt
           c.   tīme
           d.   sō
           e.   māybē
           f.   lēaf
           g.   lăugh
           h.   māne
2.020   a.   I got up early.
           b.   I got ready for school.
           c.   I had a good breakfast.
           d.   My friends and I walked to school.
           e.   The teacher was happy to see us.

SECTION 3

3.1   (James was given a place in the All City Band)
3.2   a, b, d, f, g
3.3   a.   James wanted to be like his brother.
         b.   James practiced.
         c.   James played well.
         d.   James' parents helped him.
3.4   The big zebras (ran) down the hill.
3.5   Marjorie (ran) and (skipped) all the way to school.
3.6   The teacher (shut) the door.
3.7   The dogs and cats (were) (running) and (playing) in the yard.
3.8   The baby (screamed) and (cried.)
3.9   This funny monkey (jumped) up and down.
3.10 The boys and girls (played) baseball.
3.11 Mom (turned) the light off.
3.12–3.19 Examples:
3.12 spotted
3.13 green
3.14 girl
3.15 strong
3.16 two
3.17 twelve
3.18 hard
3.19 heavy
3.20–3.27 Examples:
3.20 yesterday
3.21 never
3.22 everywhere
3.23 nearby
3.24 quickly
3.25 carefully
3.26 slowly
3.27 well
3.28 Teacher check
3.29 I have done my work today.
3.30 I have grown tomatoes in my garden.
3.31 I have sung in the choir.
3.32 I have taken my book to the library.
3.33 I have written a letter to my grandparents.
3.34 I have seen a falling star.
3.35 My sister has gone to a movie.
3.36 The teacher has given us a surprise.

3.37 (have) come
3.38 (am) hoping
3.39 (is) looking
3.40 (has) gone
3.41 (have) looked
3.42 (was) dripping
3.43 (were) burned
3.44 (has) gone
3.45 (has) paid
3.46 (have) broken
3.47 have
3.48 am or was
3.49 have
3.50 Have
3.51 has
3.52 have
3.53 Has
3.54 have
3.55 Any order:
         a.   heading
         b.   greeting
         c.   body
         d.   closing
         e.   signature
3.56 a.   752 N. 10th St.
              Phoenix, AZ 85018
              May 2, 2016
         b.   Dear Uncle Joe,
         c.   With love,
         d.   Jimmy
3.57 Teacher check
3.58 Teacher check

SELF TEST 3

3.01 Samson knew that God had a special plan for his life.

3.02
a. x
b. x
c.
d. x
e. x

3.03
a. x
b. x
c. x
d.

3.04 day, Jack, game, house, truck, bicycle, street

3.05 playing, stop, ran, saw, had come

3.06 yellow, big, delivery, new, red

3.07 quietly, suddenly, fast, quickly

3.08 is

3.09 are

3.010 was

3.011 were

3.012 am

3.013 has

3.014 have

3.015 had

3.016
a. māde
b. mēan
c. māybē

3.017
a. maĭd
b. măd
c. māne

3.018
a. mĭx
b. mīght
c. mĕt

3.019 an animal

3.020 bunch growing together

3.021 underground road

3.022 change

3.023 clear out

3.024 2

3.025 4

3.026 1

3.027 3

3.028 5

3.029 The red, yellow, blue, and green crayons are here.

3.030 What time will Suzie leave?

3.031 My Aunt Jane lives in Salem, Oregon.

3.032 The letter came on April 2, 2016.

3.033 Is Mr. E.L. Smith your neighbor?

3.034 Yes, we live in the U.S.A. now.

SECTION 4

4.1 Teacher check

4.2 stories that are not really true

4.3 yes

4.4 no

4.5 no

4.6 Teacher check

4.7 atlas

4.8 dictionary

4.9 encyclopedia

4.10 atlas

4.11 dictionary

4.12 encyclopedia

4.13 nonfiction

4.14 nonfiction

4.15 nonfiction

4.16 nonfiction

4.17 fiction

4.18 fiction

4.19 fiction

4.20 nonfiction

4.21
a. brother
b. chores
c. friends
d. morning
e. Saturday
f. tasks

4.22
a. atlas
b. Bible
c. dictionary
d. encyclopedia
e. maps
f. newspaper

4.23
a. Jacob
b. Jerusalem
c. Jesus
d. Jews
e. Joshua
f. Judah

4.24
a. Saturday
b. school
c. scored
d. she
e. someone
f. Suzie

4.25
a. baseball
b. bat
c. boys
d. brother
e. diamond
f. people
g. quarrel
h. runs

4.26
a. ability
b. army
c. catching
d. country
e. park
f. people
g. played
h. sailors
i. sat
j. skills
k. soldiers
l. sports

4.27 <u>Andrew is remembered for bringing people to Jesus</u>.

4.28 a, b, d, e

4.29 Teacher check

4.30 Teacher check

4.31 Teacher check

4.32 Teacher check

4.33 Any order:
a. ginger/bread
b. some/body
c. corn/field
d. up/stairs

4.34 Any order:
a. invited
b. ripest
c. sneezing

4.35 clapping

4.36 Any order:
a. uncover
b. remodel
c. disappear

4.37 Any order:
a. invited
b. sneezing
c. sleepless
d. fourteen
e. clapping
f. fresher
g. darkness
h. fifteen - five
i. ripest
j. coolest
k. handful

4.38 Either order:
a. veg e ta ble
b. sad dle

4.39 Examples:
a. <u>Fourteen</u> mice chased <u>fifteen</u> <u>gingerbread</u> boys <u>upstairs</u>.
b. <u>Darkness</u> covered the <u>cornfield</u> and a <u>handful</u> of ants <u>invited</u> the roaches to a feast.

SELF TEST 4

4.01 fiction
4.02 nonfiction
4.03 alphabetical order
4.04 atlas
4.05 dictionary
4.06 encyclopedia
4.07 Either order:
a. encyclopedia
b. dictionary
4.08 X
4.09
4.010 X
4.011 X
4.012 X
4.013 X
4.014
4.015 X
4.016 X
4.017 top or up
4.018 by the key or guide
4.019 what the story is all about
4.020 facts about the main idea
4.021 a. Ecclesiastes
b. Ezra
c. Genesis
d. Job
e. Judges
f. Leviticus
g. Proverbs
h. Psalms
i. Ruth
4.022 Teacher check
4.023 When will the plane leave Minot, North Dakota?
4.024 Send this package to Mrs. C.V. Brown in Pueblo, Colorado.
4.025 My brother was born on August 7, 2015.
4.026 We had hamburgers, corn, salad, brownies, and peaches for lunch.
4.027 On Tuesday, June 6, my grandmother will come to visit.
4.028 David, please be here on Sept. 6.
4.029 No, I don't think you should go.
4.030 a. skāte
b. skĭp
c. slēep
d. slīde
e. stĕm

4.031 (car) came (street)
4.032 (bicycle) is broken
4.033 (mouse) ran
4.034 (pony) trotted
4.035 (dog) barked (cat)
4.036 a. big
b. quickly
4.037 a. black
b. quietly
4.038 a. red
b. swiftly
4.039 a. tired
b. slowly
4.040 a. fat
b. loudly

Answer Keys | Language Arts 310

LIFEPAC TEST

1. Lunch was picnic
2. coats were chair
3. Mother put patch pants
4. clown made face
5. sister cooked chicken supper
6. tallest here
7. funnier fast
8. big black quickly
9. slow away
10. pretty white swiftly away
11. Sandra came to know Jesus.
12. Karen helped her friend find Jesus.
13. a. Karen asked Sandra to Sunday school.
    b. Sandra went to a Sunday school picnic.
    or Karen and her mother talked to Sandra.
14. asked to Sunday school: seeing others pray; talking to Karen and Karen's mother
15. reading for fun — atlas
16. word meanings — fiction
17. maps — dictionary
18. information — nonfiction
19. reading for facts — Or — encyclopedia
20. more than one
21. each time
22. at last
23. The yellow, white, and black cats ran.
24. X
25. On Tuesday, May 17, 2016, we will go to Austin, Texas.
26. Yes, Susan goes to Mayfield School.
27. Are Mr. and Mrs. Badin your neighbors?
28. X
29. ✓
30. ✓
31. X
32. a. wăgŏn
    b. wăll
    c. wīndōw
    d. wĭtch
    e. wŏmăn

ALTERNATE LIFEPAC TEST

1. Example:
   We went to the circus. We saw lions, tigers, elephants, and trapeze artists. We had a good time.
2. That pet (shop) sells (puppies).
   The tall (trees) at (school) swayed gently.
   May I have a chocolate (cookie)?
   The friendly (dentist) checked my (teeth) carefully.
   The kitchen (clock) stopped suddenly.
   My big (brother) can run fast.
3. Adjectives
   pet
   tall
   chocolate
   friendly
   kitchen
   big
   Adverbs
   gently
   carefully
   suddenly
   fast
4. Example:
   Bobby had to stay after school to finish his work.
5. Bobby was late for school.
6. He played around; he didn't eat; his mother got him up.
7. Example: He had to make up the work.
8. factual, true; reading for information
9. reading for fun; imaginary, made-up
10. to find something on a map
11. to find out the meaning of a word, how to spell it, and how to pronounce it
12. to find information about something
13. b ē a n
14. b ĕ a r
15. b ē a t
16. b ĕ t
17. c ē a s e
18. Robinson, Truck
19. Ruth, Babe
20. Sampras, Pete
21. Staubach, Roger
22. White, Jo Jo
23. wasted time
24. felt uneasy
25. had nothing in it

194

26.   _X_ Are Mr. and Mrs. Stuback your
       neighbors?
27.   _X_ Yes, they came here on Wednesday,
       Sept. 16, 2015.
28.   _X_ We have pink, white, yellow, and red
       roses in the yard.
29.   ___ the tall green tree
30.   _X_ Sally and Ralph go to Franklin School
       in Indianapolis, Indiana.
31.   northeast
32.   north
33.   northeast
34.   eighteen
35.   south

SPELLING TEST

1	beach	I love to swim at the **beach**.	beach
2	circle	We drew a **circle** in the dirt for our marble game.	circle
3	float	Tommy likes to **float** down the river.	float
4	guard	The Roman soldiers were told to **guard** the tomb.	guard
5	hurry	If you do not **hurry** up, we will be late.	hurry
6	knee	Bob went down on one **knee** to catch the grounder.	knee
7	maid	Most people cannot afford to hire a **maid**.	maid
8	nurse	The **nurse** took my pulse.	nurse
9	speak	It is not polite to **speak** when someone else is talking.	speak
10	write	Herman is going to **write** a letter to his pen pal.	write
11	bicycle	I ride my **bicycle** to school everyday.	bicycle
12	calves	We watched the baby **calves** trying to walk.	calves
13	ceiling	Even dad can not touch the **ceiling**.	ceiling
14	enough	I have had **enough** swimming for one day.	enough
15	everybody	**Everybody** stood up to sing the hymn.	everybody
16	frown	It is easier to smile than it is to **frown**.	frown
17	grown	I have **grown** six inches in the last year.	grown
18	leaves	We rake **leaves** in the fall.	leaves
19	neither	**Neither** Bob nor I can swim very well.	neither
20	receive	If you **receive** Christ into your heart, you will be saved.	receive
21	station	We met dad at the bus **station**.	station
22	thought	I **thought** I would score, but the goalie blocked my shot.	thought
23	vacation	Every summer we go on **vacation**.	vacation
24	coolest	The **coolest** it gets in summer is 105°.	coolest
25	darkness	**Darkness** is nothing to fear.	darkness
26	disappear	Whenever we have a test, I wish I could **disappear**.	disappear
27	fifteen	When I am **fifteen**, I can learn to drive.	fifteen
28	fresher	These apples are **fresher** than those.	fresher
29	gingerbread	We make **gingerbread** men at Christmas.	gingerbread
30	invited	Suzie **invited** me to stay all night.	invited
31	ripest	Only pick the **ripest** pears.	ripest

SPELLING TEST

32	sleepless	After the ball game, I had another **sleepless** night.	sleepless
33	somebody	Would **somebody** please close the door?	somebody
34	upstairs	My bedroom is **upstairs**.	upstairs
35	vegetable	Beans are my favorite **vegetable**.	vegetable

LANGUAGE ARTS 310

ALTERNATE LIFEPAC TEST

NAME _____

DATE _____

SCORE _____

68
—
85

Each answer = 1 point

Follow these directions.

1. Write a short essay or poem.

   _____

   _____

   _____

   _____

   _____

   _____

   _____

   _____

2. Circle each noun in these sentences. Put a line under each verb.

   a. That pet shop sells puppies.

   b. The tall trees at school swayed gently.

   c. May I have a chocolate cookie?

   d. The friendly dentist checked my teeth carefully.

   e. The kitchen clock stopped suddenly.

   f. My big brother can run fast.

3. Using the sentences in activity 2, write the adjectives and adverbs in the correct columns.

Adjectives	Adverbs
_____	_____
_____	_____
_____	_____
_____	_____
_____	
_____	

Read the paragraph. Then answer the questions.

Bobby knew he should have gotten up earlier. Now, he was going to be late for school. His mother had awakened him on time, but he had just played around and did not get dressed. He did not have time to eat any breakfast. Now, his stomach didn't feel good because he was worried and his stomach was empty. Bobby walked in the door and ...

4. What is the outcome of this paragraph?

_____

_____

5. What is the main idea?

_____

_____

6. What are the supporting details?

_____

_____

7. The causes of his being late are *fooling around* and *not getting ready for school*. What is the effect?

_____

_____

Answer these questions.

8. What is nonfiction reading?

_____

_____

9. What is fiction?

_____

_____

10. Why would you use an atlas?

_____

_____

11. Why would you use a dictionary?

_____

_____

12. Why would you use an encyclopedia?

_____

_____

Put these words in alphabetical order.
Then, mark the long and short vowels. Cross out the silent vowels.

bet   bear   cease   beat   bean

13. _____

14. _____

15. _____

16. _____

17. _____

Put these names and nicknames in alphabetical order by last name.

Babe Ruth   Roger Staubach   Pete Sampras
Jo Jo White   Truck Robinson

18. _____

19. _____

20. _____

21. _____

22. _____

Put a circle around the words at the ends of the sentences that tell what the underlined words mean.

23. Bobby had <u>played</u> around and now he was late for school.

played a joke
doesn't have sense
wasted time

24. Bobby was <u>worried</u> about being late for school.

bite at something
feel uneasy
wastes time

25. His stomach felt <u>empty</u>.

had nothing in it
poured it out
took it out

Put X in front of each complete sentence. Capitalize and punctuate correctly.

26. _____ are mr and mrs stuback your neighbors

27. _____ yes they came here on wed sept 16 2015

28. _____ we have pink white yellow and red roses in the yard

29. _____ the tall green tree

30 _____ sally and ralph go to franklin school in indianapolis indiana

Look at this map. Answer the questions.

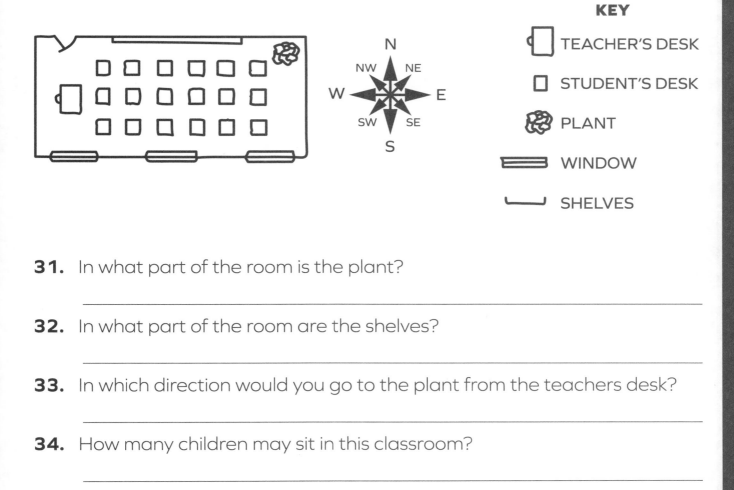

KEY

☐ TEACHER'S DESK

☐ STUDENT'S DESK

🌸 PLANT

▱ WINDOW

⌣ SHELVES

31. In what part of the room is the plant?

_____

32. In what part of the room are the shelves?

_____

33. In which direction would you go to the plant from the teachers desk?

_____

34. How many children may sit in this classroom?

_____

35. In what part of the room are the windows?

_____

ALTERNATE SPELLING TEST

1	apart	The twins looked so much alike it was hard to tell them **apart**.	apart
2	cartoon	The class laughed at the funny **cartoon** the teacher held up.	cartoon
3	fight	As Christians, we have a daily **fight** with temptations in the world.	fight
4	goat	That **goat** ate my hat!	goat
5	guard	The Roman soldiers were told to **guard** the tomb.	guard
6	herd	The cowboys drove their **herd** of cattle to Dodge City.	herd
7	knee	Bob went down on one **knee** to catch the grounder.	knee
8	knock	I heard a loud **knock** at the door.	knock
9	night	Jane reads her Bible every **night**.	night
10	perfect	Jesus was **perfect** and without sin.	perfect
11	speech	We listened to the President's **speech**.	speech
12	wrong	Hank only had one **wrong** answer on the test.	wrong
13	bicycle	I ride my **bicycle** to school everyday.	bicycle
14	bright	The **bright** sun hurt my eyes.	bright
15	calves	We watched the baby **calves** trying to walk.	calves
16	candy	Mother gave us some **candy** as a treat.	candy
17	direction	We went in the wrong **direction** and got lost.	direction
18	everybody	**Everybody** stood up to sing the hymn.	everybody
19	laugh	Funny clowns make me **laugh**.	laugh
20	leaves	We rake **leaves** in the fall.	leaves
21	neither	**Neither** Bob nor I can swim very well.	neither
22	sight	**Sight** is one of the five senses.	sight
23	taught	My brother **taught** me how to fish.	taught
24	thrown	Her clothes were **thrown** carelessly around her room.	thrown
25	clapping	The children were **clapping** in time with the music.	clapping
26	cornfield	Our cow got loose in the **cornfield**.	cornfield
27	fifteen	When I am **fifteen**, I can learn to drive.	fifteen
28	fourteen	In **fourteen** days, I leave for England.	fourteen
29	gingerbread	We make **gingerbread** men at Christmas.	gingerbread
30	handful	I ate a **handful** of strawberries.	handful

ALTERNATE SPELLING TEST

31	remodel	Mother wants to **remodel** our living room.	remodel
32	saddle	Butch showed me how to **saddle** a horse.	saddle
33	sneezing	I started **sneezing** at 3:00 and have not stopped yet!	sneezing
34	uncover	Mom decided to **uncover** the flowers.	uncover
35	vegetable	Beans are my favorite **vegetable**.	vegetable